ASPECTS OF
EIGHTEENTH CENTURY
NATURE POETRY

3.45

ASPECTS OF
EIGHTEENTH CENTURY
NATURE POETRY

C. V. DEANE

NEW   YORK

BARNES & NOBLE, INC.

Publishers · Booksellers · Since 1873

58920

Published by
FRANK CASS AND COMPANY LIMITED
67 Great Russell Street, London WC1
by arrangement with Basil Blackwell

Published in the United States
in 1968
by Barnes & Noble, Inc.
105 Fifth Avenue, New York, N.Y. 10003

LC 68-1775

First edition   1935
New impression   1968

Printed in Holland by
N. V. Grafische Industrie Haarlem

To
J.O.F.M.

PREFACE

THIS study, which was undertaken during the tenure of a Harrison Fellowship at the University of Pennsylvania, aims to provide a fresh estimate of the positive values of neo-classic and pre-romantic nature poetry. Since most of the adverse criticism of this phase of literature tends to concentrate either upon the poetic diction or the pseudo-pictorial 'composition' of descriptive poetry, an attempt has been made to arrive at a better understanding of these subjects than has prevailed hitherto. Particular emphasis has been laid, throughout the inquiry, on the need for discriminating between a lifeless and an imaginative use of conventional poetic language, and between a pictorial and a poetic sense of design.

My special thanks are due to Professor J. C. Mendenhall, of the University of Pennsylvania, for many valuable suggestions, and for the continuous interest he has taken in the progress of the work. The account of John Philips is reprinted here with the kind permission of the editor of the *Cambridge Review*.

Colchester; October 1935.   C.V.D.

CONTENTS

PART ONE

CHAPTER I

INTRODUCTORY

WHEN Wordsworth in his Essay of 1815 declared that except for the *Nocturnal Reverie* of Lady Winchilsea, and a few passages in Pope's *Windsor Forest*, the poetry of the period between *Paradise Lost* and *The Seasons* was devoid of fresh nature-imagery, and gave little indication of the poet's eye having been fixed on his object, he doubtless implied—what was clearly the case—that the poetry of the post-Thomson era was of a very different character, being detailed, wide-ranging in quest for varied effects, and copiously capable of depicting nature in either a circumstantial or a pictorial manner. But though the expression of the eloquent school differed so markedly from that of the poets who favoured the artificial style, it may be doubted whether the underlying experience, the capacity to enjoy nature, was so conspicuously poor in the earlier period as is sometimes maintained. The 'return to nature' becomes recognizable as a decisive movement from about 1750 onwards; 'Capability' Brown succeeds Kent in the sphere of landscape-gardening; Sandby, Alexander Cozens and Richard Wilson establish the growing school of landscape-painting; in poetry, Akenside, Gray, Collins and the Wartons sound a new note of lyrical intimacy; in travel-literature Dr. Brown's enthusiastic description of Keswick prepares the way for Gray's *Journal in the Lakes* and for the 'tours' of Young and Gilpin. All these men, no doubt, miss certain tracts of deeper, and some stretches of wider experience of nature, which had to await the new century before being brought to light, yet they can hardly be denied a pronounced and even peculiar faculty for perceiving and variously communicating the special atmosphere and lineaments of the English scene. In the same way, the nature-poetry of the Augustan era proper, though confined within straiter limits of expression, and scarcely venturing further afield than the country gentleman's park or its surrounding pasture-lands, is frequently as delicately decisive in its depiction of rural beauty as the poetry of the more expansive period that followed; its felicitous effects, however, require to be discerned through the vesture of conventional phraseology in which it is garbed. Many pages in Pope, Parnell, Ambrose Philips and Gay will repay close consideration from this point of view. The nature-poetry of the post-Thomson era, however, also has its derogatory label which, in spite of some recent revaluations, is too often made an excuse for the depreciatory neglect of many of its representative productions. Not only the didactic-descriptive blank verse pieces (which vary considerably in merit) but also the lyrics of poets of genuine individuality such as Shenstone, Cunningham and the Wartons, are apt to be summarily judged as on the one hand external, tediously minute, laboriously Latinized in style, and on the other as shallow, dilettante, and falsely 'poetic.' The substance of many of these disparagements is anticipated in Lessing's censure of eighteenth-century descriptive verse as a form of writing mistakenly pictorial in aim, a judgment of which we shall have more to say later, when discussing the implications of the *Laokoon*. The whole body of this nature-poetry, then, suffers from the stigma of two traditional criticisms—that in its early period it was too empty, and in its later period, if anything too full of descriptive material.

Of recent years, eighteenth-century verse has been rising nearer the level of its original valuation, while correspondingly there has been somewhat of a slump in the gilt-edged poets of later times. In the province of nature-poetry, however, there is perhaps still a tendency to mark out for special admiration those types of verse that least bear the imprint of their age. Thus Lady Winchilsea's poems—and the consummate *Nocturnal Reverie* in particular—receive renewed praise, while Akenside's lines on Wensbeck are extolled for the remarkable premonition of Wordsworth that they afford. In regard to the last-named example, it seems that a juster attitude to take would be that adopted by Professor Elton, who observes that

> *Tintern Abbey* . . . from one point of view is the fine flower of
> eighteenth-century meditative poetry. In Akenside and Thomson
> there are clear traces of an intimate, rapturous feeling for natural

beauty, and also the sense of 'something far more deeply inter-
fused.'[1]

The present study has been undertaken in the belief that
there is room for a defence of the nature-verse of the
eighteenth century that may be considered as wholly typical
of its age and that such a defence need not concern itself unduly with poems that belong to literary history rather than to
literature. A rehabilitation of this kind will almost inevitably
take the form of an attempt to lessen the force of the two
main charges against this poetry—first, that poetic diction,
both the Popian and the neo-Miltonic kind, has an almost
invariably deadening effect on nature-verse, where it is
chiefly found; and secondly that the poetry of the elo-
quently descriptive school, from Thomson onwards, shows
an over-indulgence in dispersive detail which is the outcome
of a mistaken attempt to rival the art of the landscape-
painter.

Until we come to examine the work of some selected
poets in detail, these two aspects of the subject will be
treated separately; though they are associated in so far as
the effective symmetry of poetic diction and the just arrangement of descriptive material both betoken the beneficent
influence of neo-classic ideals of form and design.[2]   Nevertheless it is doubtful whether they are so closely connected
as they are alleged to be by Professor Irving Babbitt, who
contends (*The New Laokoon*, p. 18 sq.) that poetic diction
arose from the identification of poetry and painting produced
by a *literal* acceptance of the 'ut pictura poesis' doctrine. In
his special pleading for a hypothetical 'humanism' which is
averred to exist midway between the extremes of the neo-
classicists' objective confusion of the arts (in terms of
painting) and the romanticists' subjective confusion of
them (frequently in terms of music), Professor Babbitt may
be held to have unduly simplified the neo-classical philosophy
of art, especially as regards the relation of theory to practice.
We may admit that the theory of imitation was carried to
undue lengths in neo-classic times, and yet demur at the
notion that a consciousness of the formula 'words resemble
colours,' in the sense of poetical colouring to be laid on like

[1] *The English Muse*, p. 311.
[2] For further remarks on this topic, see pp. 50, 61-2.

pigments from without—to whatever degree this idea may have been entertained by a few post-Renaissance critics—was the motive that impelled the poets to plunder Spenser and Milton for useful or ornamental phrases and epithets. There would seem to be no reason why we should not rest content with the traditional and purely literary explanation of the rise of poetic diction—as a movement towards regularizing and refining poetic speech that was begun in France by Malherbe and encouraged in England by the practice of Waller, Denham and Dryden; a process whereby a correct 'middle style' was drawn from the cultivated conversation of the day, and a treasury of ornamental expressions was culled from the best authors of earlier times, with newly-invented expressions conforming to the types thus established.

And yet from the point of view of our present inquiry it would be preferable to regard eighteenth century poetic diction as producing an effect of fluency rather than of restraint.   No one would deny that the adoption of stock diction generally imparts an easy movement to verse, even though it may be the motion of those who are contemptuously described as having

> . . . sway'd about upon a rocking horse,
> And thought it Pegasus.

But as regards the fertilizing influence of set phraseology on the verse of the age, it may be recalled that even Wordsworth admitted that 'this language was received as a natural language; and at length, by the influence of books upon men, did to a certain degree really become so.'[1] There are certain indubitable virtues in the prevalence of a conventional style at a time when a new range of poetic subject-matter presents itself. The first half of the eighteenth century, it should be remembered, saw the origin of the poetical study of nature for its own sake; a scene was neither depicted, as in the romantic era, for the sake of the emotions that could be evoked from it, nor, as in some twentieth-century verse, for the unusual patterns of words and sounds that it might suggest. The adoption of the Miltonic style coincided with what is usually called the 'return to nature,' but might be

[1] *Preface to Lyrical Ballads*, Appendix on 'Poetic Diction.'

more justly termed the enlarged view of nature, consequent on Thomson's opening up of new areas of observation for poetic treatment. Both the poets who cultivated blank verse didactics and the '*Il Penseroso* School' found themselves in a favourable position for the practising of their art; extensive new themes awaited exploration, and a mature but not yet overworked poetic language was at hand which would satisfy most of the neo-classic requirements of order, fitness, and harmonious numbers. Even during the earlier Augustan period, when the concerns of the town predominated in literature as in life, an awakened interest in nature shows itself in Pope's and Addison's rejection of the formal parterre in favour of the freer style of gardening—as exemplified in Pope's (eagerly-emulated) experiments with his five acres at Twickenham—no less than in poems such as *Windsor Forest*, Parnell's *Hermit*, Gay's *Rural Sports*, and others where pastoral or parkland scenery and rural manners are depicted with appreciative artistry. Here again the confidence induced by the existence of a stock diction that could be drawn on at will may be considered a poetical asset; the performer was free to play whatever new tunes he wished when the technique of his instrument was so secure. His lot was enviable compared to that of some present-day poets, who cannot afford to let 'pure description take the place of sense' and whose words have to be chosen with excruciating care. The Augustan poet was not inhibited, and the conventional style enabled him to recreate his experiences with the less fear of lapsing into preciosity on the one hand or banality on the other. That he did sometimes incur the latter mischance is, of course, notorious, and the art of calling a spade by some other name, such as

> Metallic Blade, wedded to ligneous Rod
> Wherewith the rustic Swain upturns the Sod

led the eighteenth-century bard into kindred inventions— 'lucid orbs,' 'gelid cistern' and the like—which are only less remarkable than the above-quoted example of circumlocution in excelsis from Erasmus Darwin's *Botanic Garden*.

Apart from the prevalence of obvious blemishes such as these, and the misuse of Personification, which is equally prominent, one of the chief reasons for the disparagement of early eighteenth-century nature verse is that while the 'objects' of description are numerous, the style is sedulously restricted, so that it might be (and no doubt has been) likened to the monotonous tinkling of a musical-box. The variety and delicacy of modulation of which the heroic couplet was capable in the hands of its chief executant, however, have recently been revealed with telling effect by Miss Sitwell, and it will be worth inquiring whether this 'musical finesse' was used in the realm of nature-poetry by Pope and the abler poets of his school to supply by suggestion what was lacking in detailed description. It is, we surmise, because the appeal to the senses of a scene described by means of stock phraseology is less direct than that conveyed by a period landscape-painting just as circumscribed in its conventions (a Wilson, for example, with formal balancing of masses, and green trees foiled by brown shades[1]) that impatience with the former medium is more likely to bar the way to appreciation. In our attitude to the descriptive style of the artificial school something more than suspended judgement is required; for the larger part of the stock embellishments employed do not produce an effect of falsity, they are solely chargeable with being tediously stereotyped, and with these it will frequently reward us to inquire whether the given phrase has not been used deliberately (rather than mechanically) like the brown shade of a contemporary landscape-painter, in order to contribute—in terms of aural composition—to a satisfying harmony of design. Aural composition is to be seen to best advantage in the pastoral poetry of the period, where, since the imagery is narrow in range and the epithets are mostly abstract, the effect of the poem is liable to depend more on the arrangement and skilful interplay of familiar sound-and-sense expressions than on freshness and novelty of sentiment. It is to be distinguished from visual composition, which may be defined as the means whereby the poet (usually of the Thomson school) arranges the objects of his scene so as to present to the imaginative eye of the reader a convincing and comprehensive view of the landscape;

---

[1]Where, o'er the rock, the scarcely waving pine
Fills the brown shade with a religious awe.
THOMSON, *Hymn*, 43.

a method which, since it is often alleged to be ineffectually imitative of landscape-painting, will receive a separate and detailed investigation in later chapters.

PERSONIFICATION AND ABSTRACTION

As to that other feature of poetic diction, the device of abstraction and personification, less can be said in its favour, though somewhat less need be said about it, since the practice is on the whole not as prevalent in nature-poetry as in other kinds of verse, such as the moral epistle and the meditative or panegyrical ode. The harmfulness of its effect may be indicated by saying that whereas the circumlocutions and stock epithets used by the better poets are for the most part endowed with some animation or quality of musical suggestion, the personified abstractions employed by them are apt to be stiff and rhetorical as often as vital and suggestive. In order to give some support to the latter assertion, let us draw a few illustrations from prominent writers of nature-poems during the century.

We may point, for example, to the catalogue of evils, represented at the end of *Windsor Forest* as banished to deepest hell by 'fair Peace'—'barbarous Discord,' 'pale Terror,' 'gloomy Care,' and the like—as being one of the chief disfigurements of the poem, on account of its emptily rhetorical character. To the same class may be assigned Thomson's list of merely melodramatic personifications in *Spring* (282 sq.).

> Senseless and deformed,
> Convulsive anger storms at large; or, pale
> And silent, settles into fell revenge.
> Base envy withers at another's joy. . . .

an enumeration of the ills which have afflicted society since the vanishing of the golden age. Thomson, however, has several better examples, where the attention is not riveted to the posture and stage properties of the personification, but is encouraged to dilate and fill in the scene with the colours of fancy. Thus in *Summer* we have the description of a dawn

> The meek-eyed Morn appears, mother of dews
> At first faint-gleaming in the dappled east

and at the opening of the same poem, another personification of movement and gradual change which, if less striking in isolation, is equally effective in its context and its reference to the preceding poem :

> He [Summer] comes attended by the sultry hours
> And ever-fanning breezes, on his way;
> While, from his ardent look, the turning Spring
> Averts her blushing face.

The intensive cult of Milton's early poems may be held responsible for the abundance of abstractions in the odes and lyrics of the Warton brothers, but for the most part the attributes of their personifications, like the poorer ones of Pope and Thomson illustrated above, consist of lifelessly conventionalized epithets. Thus a plentiful assortment of phrases such as 'soft Pity,' 'Superstition blind,' 'wan Indolence' is to be found in Thomas Warton's quatrains *Written at Vale Abbey*, while Joseph's *Enthusiast, or the Lover of Nature*, in other respects a very fair specimen of his talent, contains the following procession of seedy effigies:

> next, virgin Solitude
> Serene, who blushes at each gazer's sight;
> Then Wisdom's hoary head, with crutch in hand,
> Trembling, and bent with age; last, Virtue's self,
> Smiling, in white array'd, who with her leads
> Sweet Innocence, that prattles by her side,
> A naked boy!

Gray's personifications, about which we shall have more to say in a later connection, are generally of the pretentiously statuesque type, but we may note here that he sometimes vitalizes his figures by depicting them as moving and acting, rather than in attitudes of self-exhibition. The vigorous stroke in the *Hymn to Adversity* whereby Laughter, Noise and Folly are represented as being

> By vain Prosperity received,
> To her they vow their truth, and are again believed

may be compared in this respect to some of the more dynamic personifications in Collins's *Ode to the Passions*.

Though the latter piece contains examples of the tiresomely artificial kind, Collins's poetry may in general be held to provide the outstanding excuse for the prevalence of the figure in eighteenth-century verse. The number of his odes that are addressed to abstractions is remarkable, even allowing for the fashion of the time. It is evident that he had an inborn and peculiar gift for significantly visualizing abstract conceptions—a quality that can be immediately perceived in an example such as

> Long pity, let the nations view
> Thy sky-worn robes of tender blue
> And eyes of dewy light

from the *Ode to Pity*—together with an almost mythological instinct for personifying properties of nature. His skill in portraying evanescent and transitory effects of natural beauty by unobtrusively varying the attributes of his central figure is seen at its best in the *Ode to Evening*, where, as Mr. Edmund Blunden has nicely observed, the 'maid composed' is successively revealed to us as 'a country girl, a Fairy Queen, a priestess, a goddess, a ghost in the sky.' Yet even in this acknowledged masterpiece it is difficult to avoid looking askance at the cluster of abstractions—'fancy, friendship, science, rose-lipped health'—which tail off the poem. We may be almost persuaded by Mr. Blunden that 'the watcher and the humanities and solitudes which he contemplates are all subjects of that "quiet rule"' and yet remain half-resentful at the too easy inroads into this magical atmosphere on the part of figures that would be equally at home in a more public and unelusive association. The passage seems to occupy an uneasy border-position between genuine and derivative utterance on account of its over-ready admittance of these amphibious fictions beneath the shelter of the 'sylvan shed.'

The comparative frequency with which the writers of shorter nature-poems in the eighteenth century amplify their endings by resorting to the device of *prosopopoeia* has not, we think, been previously noticed. The tendency is to be seen in both famous and less well-known examples; thus besides the closing lines of Collins's ode, we have the figures of 'fair science' and 'melancholy' in the Epitaph of Gray's *Elegy*, the personifications of 'Quiet' and 'Pleasure' at the conclusion of *Grongar Hill*, and the dismissal of the group of evils, before-mentioned, with which Pope rounds off *Windsor Forest*. The Wartons emulate their more gifted brethren in this as in other respects; thus Thomas Warton's freshest poem *The First of April* ends with a vision of Ceres, June, and Plenty, while Joseph's *Ode to Evening* concludes, probably in deliberate contrast to Collins's slightly earlier ode on the same theme, with an enumeration of the passions allayed by evening's calming influence—'desponding Love,' 'pining Envy,' 'Anger and mad Ambition.' It is as if the didactic element, temporarily held in check, but (owing largely to the influence of the 'ethical' school of Pope) never far away in the verse of the age, waits for a favourable moment to reassert itself. Yet the *coda* of personifications cannot be entirely accounted for in this way, since many of the figures have the appearance of being introduced more for decorative than instructive purposes. The underlying function of the latter, however, is rather that of presenting the strange in terms of the familiar, for the observed facts of nature were new poetic territory, which had to be brought under the sway of prevailing general conceptions for the benefit of the contemporary reader. Thus whereas the Romantic nature-poet does not usually regard the experience as valid until he relates it to his *personal* emotions and aspirations, his eighteenth-century predecessor though he may have felt the objective experience to be complete in itself, was impelled to relate it to *universal* ideas—a process which involved rounding it off with the aid of the rationalistic abstractions of his day—in order to make it acceptable to his audience.

It has been suggested that these abstractions sometimes had a spiritual or pantheistic significance for the poets who used them; that they expressed a sense of the 'animation of what philosophers were vainly trying to persuade them (the poets) was the machine of nature.'[1] The theory is attractive, and has a certain colour lent to it by some of the observations of the nature-loving philosophers of the time, as is shown for

[1] *T.L.S.*, November 10, 1927.

example in the description of the 'deep shades of a vast wood' by Shaftesbury:

> Here Space astonishes, Sense itself seems pregnant; whilst an unknown Force works on the Mind, and dubious Objects move on the wakeful sense. Mysterious voices are either heard or fancy'd; and various Forms of Deity seem to present themselves, and appear more manifest in these sylvan Scenes; such as of old gave rise to Temples, and favour'd the Religion of the ancient World.

But while we may allow that there was a tendency for the 'religion of nature' to become a creed among poets such as Akenside and Thomson, it is doubtful whether—except for isolated examples in these poets—the direct form of personification was often used to this end. In the majority of instances, it is preferable to regard the device as something manifestly ornamental, capable at times of conjuring up delectable scenes and shifting colours by the power of suggestion, but more often apt to burden otherwise felicitous nature-poems with a chill effect of generalization and conventional rhetoric.

STOCK IMAGERY: POETIC PERIPHRASES

We have dwelt on the subject of personification partly lest it be thought that in the ensuing pages, where the attempt is made to restore poetic diction to favour as a vehicle of nature-poetry, the case is overstated, and insufficient attention is paid to the less defensible aspects of the practice. If however only a few pre-eminent poets succeeded in using the device of personification imaginatively, it may be claimed that a considerably larger number of writers turned the poetic periphrasis to good account. Yet this convention has received as much defamation at the hands of critics as has the former, ranging from Coleridge's admiring recollection of his schoolmaster's admonitions—'Harp? Harp? Lyre? Pen and ink, boy, you mean! Muse, boy,

Muse? Your nurse's daughter, you mean! Pierian spring?
Oh aye! the cloister-pump, I suppose!'—to the scathing
comments of that modern Romantic critic, Raleigh, on the
eighteenth-century imitators of Milton:

> Milton's shadowy grandeur, his avoidance of plain concrete
> terms, his manner of linking adjective with substantive, were all
> necessary to him for the describing of his strange world; but
> these . . . became a mere vicious trick of absurd periphrasis and
> purposeless vagueness for description of common and familiar
> objects. A reader making his first acquaintance with Thomson's
> *Seasons* might suppose that the poem was written for a wager, to
> prove that country life may be described, and nothing called by
> its name.

Judgements of this type, it is scarcely necessary to remon-
strate, err through a failure to discriminate between the
mechanical and the suggestive use of the conventional phrase,
through a reluctance to perceive that in the better poets'
adoption of the latter

> Far the greatest part
> Of what some call neglect, is study'd art.

It is true that it would be difficult to find a passage in
eighteenth-century verse that, for power of soaring into the
higher regions of song by means of commonplace nature-
imagery, could compare with Milton's:

> but chief
> Thee, Sion, and the flowery brooks beneath,
> That wash thy hallowed feet and warbling flow.

But the raptly contemplative quality of the passage that
contains these lines is conditioned by a subject very different
in character to that of the descriptive nature-poem, and the
triumphs of this kind of poetry should not be allowed to
obscure the claims of less adventurous compositions.
Among the latter, we frequently find instances where trite
and original images are joined together, such as the following, from Shenstone's *Rural Elegance*:

> The habitual scene of hill and dale,
> The rural herds, the vernal gale,
> The tangled vetch's purple bloom,
> The fragrance of the bean's perfume.

The evident capacity for detailed observation disclosed in

these lines should at least cause us to ask whether the mingling of fresh and stock imagery has not been deliberately sought after, in order to convey an agreeably diffused effect—such as is apt to persist when amidst the placid and mellow profusion of an English pastoral landscape, the attention is arrested by some transiently striking scent or colour. This faculty for grafting original phrases on to the common stock appears in many of the better poets of the period, particularly in the work of John Philips and Thomson. A quotation from *Summer* (480–5) will illustrate Thomson's ability in this direction:

> Around the adjoining brook that purls along
> The vocal grove, now fretting o'er a rock
> Now scarcely moving through a reedy pool,
> Now starting to a sudden stream, and now
> Gently diffused into a limpid plain,—

Here the function of the stereotyped poeticisms in the first two lines is to provide a flowing musical undercurrent against which the delicate depiction of the ever-changing appearances of the brook may be seen in clearer relief.

Circuitous phrases, however, require to be recognized not merely as providing a foil to more vivid expressions, but as having poetic value in themselves. In nature-poetry perhaps the largest class comprises the roundabout designations of the various species of the animal kingdom. This usage is often singled out by critics as being particularly pompous and inanimate; thus Raleigh charges Thomson with the fabrication of 'some dozen devices for escaping from the flat vulgarity of calling birds by that name.' But such an imputation is, to say the least of it, misleading, for the minute and careful attention which Thomson devotes to the habits of the 'plumy people' shows him to have been an enthusiastic field naturalist; one of the type preferred by Gilbert White, who take their 'observations from the subject itself, and not from the writings of others.' It is true that he is uncertain whether the swallow hibernates in these islands or is a bird of passage (*Autumn* 840–8); many years later, however, the same question baffled the persistent inquiries of so zealous an ornithologist as White himself. But he notices swallows in flight during nesting-time snatching wisps of wool from the backs of sheep, he sees the covey 'watchful every way' furtively basking in the autumn stubble, he observes how bird-song subsides in the heat of a summer noon, till

The stock-dove only through the forest coos,[1]

he depicts the ruses with which the plover and wild duck divert the intruder from their nests, and, by means of choice words and skilfully-distributed sounds and stresses he vividly portrays the half-hovering homeward flight of rooks:

Retiring from the downs, where all day long
They picked their scanty fare, a blackening train
Of clamorous rooks thick-urge their weary flight,
And seek the closing shelter of the grove.

With evidence such as these (and many other) examples afford of Thomson's capacity for sharing in the concerns of wild life, there is a decided presumption against his having used the periphrasis in an external or perfunctory manner. As to passages in which birds are named, we have only to turn to the long section of *Spring* (590–788) devoted to the doings of the various species in this season, where there is material enough to satisfy the most pedestrian of annotators, in order to prove groundless the notion that he recoiled from plain names out of false gentility.

Circuitous phrases which have specific value in themselves may be divided into three main types. The largest class includes all those expressions which evoke a sense of friendly companionship between human and other forms of life. It is true that among these the more hackneyed phrases, such as 'the finny race' and 'feathered throng,' require some support from a context of appropriate spirit and tone; thus the latter expression takes on a tinge of affectionate familiarity in the following lines from Matthew Green's *The Spleen*, where the author describes his ideal country retreat:

From Eurus, foe to kitchen ground,
Fenced by a slope with bushes crowned,
Fit dwelling for the feathered throng,
Who pay their quit-rents with a song.

Similarly the infectious zest which pervades the trout-fishing episode in Thomson's *Spring* (394–442) helps to

[1]A phenomenon which the present writer chanced to witness from 'Thomson's Seat' in the woods of Hagley.

clear its periphrasis 'the finny race' of any merely rhetorical association. Not infrequently, however, we meet with variants which by their freshness and ingenuity have the power of communicating the element of sympathy independently of their contexts. Dryden's 'the trading citizens,' for bees, and Somerville's 'the jolly clan,' for a pack of hounds, are instances of the kind, while Thomson, who has a special aptitude for such coinages, gives us 'the soft fearful people,' for sheep, and (of particular charm) 'the tender race,' for bees. A more limited class comprises what may be called accurate circumlocutions, applicable in the realm of animal life to phrases remarkable for the delicate veracity with which they bring into prominence the habits and prevailing disposition of a particular species. It would not be easy to find an example of this kind comparable in merit to Cowper's characterization of sparrows as 'the pert voracious kind'; a phrase which in its happy intimacy calls to mind Keats's 'if a sparrow comes before my window, I take part in its existence and pick about the gravel.' But instances such as Bloomfield's 'chirping brood,' for young chickens, and Goldsmith's

> The sober herd that lowed to meet their young

have something of the same realistic quality. In the third group we may place periphrases which have the property of visual suggestiveness, and which secure their effects either independently, in terms of action and movement, or else by contributing to the appearance of some momentarily-glimpsed landscape. Among examples of the latter kind, pride of place should be given to Pope's

> Pour'd o'er the whitening vale their fleecy care,

from the first Pastoral, where he skilfully contrives that amidst the general atmosphere of morning brightness the stock phrase shall introduce the ideas of spaciousness and dispersion. The merits of this use of the image were evidently perceived by Gay, for in his first poem *Rural Sports*, which was dedicated to Pope, he introduced the phrase with similar effect:

> And happy shepherds, who secure from fear,
> On open downs preserve your fleecy care!

The same epithet employed in another periphrasis, in

Thomson's *Winter*, conjures up a whole skyscape of congregating snow-laden clouds:

> Heavy they roll their fleecy world along.

A similar circumlocution introduced into Crabbe's precisely-etched picture of a stretch of fen country gives an added touch of desolation to the scene:

> Birds, save a wat'ry tribe, the district shun,
> Nor chirp among the reeds where bitter waters run.

From Thomson also we may quote examples, such as 'the feathered eddy,' for a flight of swallows disporting themselves, and 'the fearful, flying race,' for a herd of deer, which have the capacity of bringing movement vividly before the eye.[1]

All these instances are (to say the least) free from the more modern poetic vice of 'particularity without experience'; for their authors take more pains to conceal and transmute than is ordinarily taken to display the results of detailed observation. And as the particularization of these poets, when it appears, is almost always the fruit of a genuine intercourse with nature, so it will be frequently found that their generalizations are apt to be backed by experience. Many of the latter, it is true, do not have the virtues (which are conspicuous as soon as they are revealed) of the examples given above, but among the better poets even the more nondescript circumlocutions may sometimes be justified as playing a part in the extended visual or musical harmony of a verse paragraph or stanza. Thus the imagery of the stanza from the *Castle of Indolence* beginning

> Joined to the prattle of the purling rills
> Were heard the lowing herds along the vale

consists entirely of 'spurious' poeticisms, but in its effect the passage is a miniature pastoral symphony, composed of uncloying skilfully-interwoven melodies. Further exemplification of this kind of artistry may be best left till we come to examine the work of a few selected poets in detail.

---

[1]Vividness is also obtainable in the mock-heroic vein by means of circumlocution. Gay's roundabout phrase for 'wig', in his *Trivia*, is a particularly happy example:
> Lurks the sly boy; whose hand, to rapine bred,
> Plucks off the curling honours of thy head.

When we contemplate the nature poems of the eighteenth century which reach artistic finality and are characteristic of their period, we may not unjustifiably surmise that the Romantic rejection of the older style was sometimes brought about more by a desire to exploit the widened resources of poetic expression than by a repugnance to the conventional phraseology of a bygone age. An analogous distinction may be made with regard to the corresponding revolution in landscape-painting wrought by Constable and Turner at the opening of the nineteenth century. Constable's refusal to include the conventional brown shade in his pictures may well have been due to his desire to reveal the beauties of rapidly-changing atmospheric effects more than to an aversion to the brown shade as such. We have to reckon with a larger palette on the one hand, and a more extensive vocabulary on the other. But while we may admit the great advance in both range and penetration that was achieved during the Romantic era, we shall do well to recognize that nature-poetry, like landscape painting, lost something valuable in the process of development.

For the authentic poets of the earlier century manifest a keen and genuine delight in the sloping lawns and glades and distant classical porticoes, the overhanging rocks and cascades and umbrageous masses of monumental trees that form the material of their characteristic pieces; and they show an enviable realization, due to their innate sense of design, of the maximum variety of effects obtainable from judicious combinations of these relatively few 'objects.' Moreover the very limitations of their descriptive technique enabled them to depict scenes of this type with a suavity and completeness which may be the more valued in that the secret of the art appears to have vanished. The country, too, with its serene aspect, extensive rural cultivation, and well tended landscape-gardens lent itself to the eulogies of poets in a way that has since been hampered by the relentless encroachments of industry and traffic. 'If wood, water, vallies, glades, can inspire a poet or a painter, this is the country, this is the age, to produce them' wrote Horace Walpole in his *Essay on Gardening* of 1771. It was a joyful vaunt, but his words were truer than he knew.

We have attempted by means of some choice examples to

predispose the reader in favour of poetic diction, but since the prejudice against it may not be so easily overcome, it will probably be advisable to approach the subject somewhat more deliberately, and by means of a few comparisons drawn from the poetic practice of earlier times, to try to establish the view that there is nothing inherently vicious in the prevalence of a markedly conventional verse-vocabulary, and that an artificial style, if artistically managed, is capable of yielding effects of absolute poetic merit.

CHAPTER II

The Diction of the Scottish Chaucerians

IN looking for comparisons between the conventional phraseology of the poetry of the eighteenth century and that of other periods, it may prove fruitful to glance for a while at the 'aureate' language of the Scottish Chaucerians, since this diction has two properties which are commonly held to be characteristic defects of the verse of the later age; the one being that its vocabulary is largely Latin in origin, and the other that it is almost entirely ornamental in purpose. It is sometimes maintained that the aureate terms derive as much from French as from Latin, but except in the rare instances where the etymological origin of such terms can be proved to be French alone, this attribution would seem to be prompted by knowledge of the fact that during the period between Bannockburn and Flodden .the cultural ties between Scotland and France were strong, and that Scotsmen who studied outside their own country usually did so in France. At French universities, however, the teaching was conducted entirely in Latin, while it is worth recalling that Dunbar, who visited France on at least two occasions, uses few words of French origin, but falls naturally into Latin in composing many of the refrains of his lyrics. Words formed from Latin stems are used to supply the profusion of internal rhymes in Dunbar's *Ballat of Our Lady*, in which poem the persistent tones of praise echo as from the vaults and arches of an abbey church:

> Hale, sterne superne! Hale, in eterne,
> In Godis sicht to schyne!
> Lucerne in derne for to discerne
> Be glory and grace devyne;
> Hodiern, modern, sempitern,
> Angelicall regyn!
> Our tern infern for to dispern
> Helpe, rialest rosyne.
> Ave Maria, gracia plena!

This poem is an extreme example of aureation, but while it is easy to condemn the piece, and others that resemble it—

such as certain stanzas in Douglas's *Palice of Honour*—as a riot of verbal extravagance, it should be remembered that in a literary period of conscious craftsmanship, of 'rethorike' and 'lusty fresch endyte' when Latin was both an indispensable language for the cultured classes, and an inexhaustible mine for the 'makaris' who wished to 'overgild' their 'speche that imperfyte stude,' the aureate terms appeared far less cumbrous and affected than they do to-day.

Scottish writers have always shown a fondness—perhaps it might more justly be called a weakness—for sonorous-sounding Latinisms; and there is little doubt that Boswell's admiration for Johnson, to take a conspicuous example, was stimulated by the great man's power to wield sentences fully charged with borrowings from the language of Rome. The extent to which a mannered and elaborate style was accepted in its own day as a customary mode of expression should be taken into account before passing judgement on its products; an exertion of the historical sense in this direction is necessary in order to enable the poetry to have its intended effect. This consideration has its bearing also on the poetry of the neo-classic age, for even the strongest opponents of poetic diction, such as Coleridge and Wordsworth, testify to the fact that the 'trade in classic niceties' was maintained by the extensive eighteenth-century practice of writing Greek and Latin verse at school. Coleridge, it is true, draws a distinction between the fifteenth century 'when the use of the Latin tongue was so general among learned men, that Erasmus is said to have forgotten his native language'[1] and the closing years of the eighteenth century, when youths composed their Latin verses with the aid of a gradus, but it is hardly a just comparison to match the highest achievement of one with the 'prentice work of the other. The poetic diction of the eighteenth century was encouraged by a closer familiarity with the classics than we can pretend to nowadays; and there is little doubt that the poets (as distinguished from the poetasters) were as aware of the felicitous effects won by Virgil and Horace by a judicious use of the classical equivalents of the stock phraseology as they were skilled in manipulating the latter themselves.

The Scots Chaucerians, however, were for the purposes

[1] *Biographia Literaria,* chapter I.

of their own verse more interested in the Latin language than in Latin literature; their aim was to dignify their idiomatic and over-emphatic vernacular (the Northumbrian dialect of Anglo-Saxon) by an abundant grafting of rich and resonant words of Latin origin. This blended style was used chiefly for allegory and the poetry of courtly compliment, and what Chaucer had begun by means of a Latin vocabulary taken through the French, his Scottish disciples carried further by drawing on the Latin direct. In translating from the classics, however, the use of the ornate style was more hazardous, and Gavin Douglas in his rendering of the *Aeneid* instinctively preferred the 'hamely termes familyar' of his own language to the artificial style of court poetry. He avoids the 'polyst terms' (which by his time were numerous and ready to hand) except when in difficulties, but frankly admits that

> the ryme
> Causes me to mak digressioun sum tyme.

The chief fault of his version is its diffuseness, and it is difficult to determine whether he had any appreciation of the weighty brevity of Virgil's line, for the prolixity of the vernacular medium inevitably prevented the reproduction of this quality. Often however he is nearer the spirit of the original than many of the correcter translators of later times, and it will be readily seen that in a passage such as the following, where Aeneas starts back at seeing the ghost of Creusa

> Abaisit I wolx, and widdersyns start my hair,
> Speik mycht I nocht, the voce in my hals sa stak

he is infinitely more expressive with his dialect words than when, for instance, he attempts to glorify Honour by means of 'rethorik' and florid imported imagery:

> For hie renoun thow art guerdon condign . . .
> Haill rois maist chois till clois thy fois greit micht,
> Haill stone quhilk schone upon the throne of licht.

As to the æsthetic value of this ornamental diction, there is a fairly marked division of opinion among writers on the subject. Among some it is maintained that the imagery is the outcome of an undue admiration for the traditional allegorical description of the May morning—with its accompanying dream, model garden, and personified abstractions—which first appeared in English in the translation (by Chaucer or another) of *The Romaunt of the Rose.* The Chaucerians carried this type of description to excessive lengths, and aimed at embellishing what was already lavish in ornament. It is alleged that a style of decadence resulted, and that apart from rare exceptions the diction was gaudy, flamboyant, and over-'enamelled', while the favourite mediaeval catalogues of bright objects were worked to death. Other writers, however, incline to the view that the aureate style is frequently a thing of beauty, but that to be truly effective it requires to be set in its surrounding element of vigorous Northern vernacular. While there is little doubt that the contrast between the harsh and the mellifluous enhances the total effect of several poems produced by this school, for the purpose of keeping in view the analogy with the artificial diction of the eighteenth century, it is preferable to inquire here whether certain aureate descriptions cannot stand in their own right, and if they can, to examine how they succeed in doing so.

As a first example let us take from Dunbar's *Goldyn Targe* a passage which is often admired for its depiction of an unusually observed natural phenomenon, the glittering reflection of light cast by dimpling water on the foliage of overhanging branches:

> Downe throu the ryce a ryvir ran wyth stremys,
> So lustily agayn thai lykand lemys,
> That all the lake as lamp did leme of licht,
> Quhilk schadowit all about wyth twynkling glemis;
> That bewis bathit war in secund bemys
> Throu the reflex of Phebus visage brycht.

Though it may be maintained that the effulgent quality of this skilfully composed and melodious description is enhanced by the elaborate diction brought into play, it is difficult to avoid the feeling that the scene could have been better suggested in simpler and fewer words. In order to exhibit passages which attain poetic finality because of, rather than in spite of their aureation, it is preferable to select such as possess some simple emotional appeal or those whose effect depends on the joyful heaping up of jewelled compliments. Henryson's *Testament of Cresseid* provides many instances of the former type of successful elaboration, and we may quote a stanza from the 'Complaint' where the aureation intensifies the contrast between the happiness of Cresseid's earlier life and her present plight:

> Quhair is thy chalmer wantounlie besene,
> With burely bed and bankouris browderit bene,
> Spycis and wyne to thy collatioun,
> The cowpis all of gold and silver schene,
> The sweit meitis, servit in plaittis clene,
> With saipheron sals of ane gud sessoun
> Thy gay garmentis with mony gudely goun,
> Thy plesand lawn pinnit with goldin prene?
> All is areir, thy greit royall renoun.

For skilful management of the other type of aureation, the apparently reckless multiplication of shining epithets, Dunbar must be given the palm, and the confident flamboyance of

> Gemme of all joy, jasper of jocunditie
> Most myghty carbuncle of vertue and valour;

in the eulogy on London, and the richly transfiguring quality of the imagery in *The Golden Targe*, as may be illustrated in the lines

> Up sprang the goldyn candill matutyne,[1]
> With clere depurit bemes cristallyne

are enough in themselves to show how poetic splendour of language can emerge from sheer ornament.

The work of the aureating poets bears a marked resemblance to that of the almost contemporaneous Florentine painters of the school of Fra Angelico; the latter copiously gild and bejewel their pictures of angels and madonnas, yet seldom so as to obscure the delicacy of outline and gracefulness of poise on which the harmony of their compositions depends. In their passion for adornment they sometimes go to the length of raising the haloes and other emblems of their figures above the surface of the pictures, the raised portion in its turn being decorated with patterns in relief. Something of this double artificiality, this superimposing of ornament upon ornament, is occasionally to be met with in Dunbar, but from a specimen such as the following:

[1] Cf. the Anglo-Saxon poetic phrase for 'the sun', *heofon condel.*

And lusty May, that muddir is of flouris,
Had maid the birdis to begyn thair houris
Among the *tendir odouris reid and quhyt*,
Quhois armony to heir it wes delyt,

it will be seen that the effect is one of happy audacity rather than of naïve bedizening, and the condensation of imagery produces a livelier impression of floral perfection than is ordinarily found in mediaeval descriptions of May mornings. Another device much favoured by the Scottish Chaucerians for the purpose of securing a pleasant surface decoration is the poetic catalogue, and their frank acceptance of it as a thing of artifice rather than as an array of carefully apt symbols prevents the prolixity of the convention from becoming oppressive.

The following example, from Dunbar's *The Thrissil and the Rois*, provides a typical list of attributes:

Welcome to be our princess of honour,
Our perle, our plesans, and our paramour,
Our peax, our play, our plane felicite. . . .

Since the aim of the catalogue is to produce an attractive surface pattern, its merit should be determined according to whether the total effect is not obscured by over-virtuosity and profusion of imagery. Dunbar, we should be inclined to say, stands the test well in this respect; in the full-dress court poems his enrichment is seldom excessive, and an artistic control may be discerned in the midst of his verbal exuberance.

As regards the bearings on eighteenth-century verse of the foregoing remarks, it may be objected that no very serviceable comparison can be drawn between the two kinds of diction, since the style of one is gothic, while that of the other is rococo; in the latter we find a well-worn 'system of words', whereas the metaphorical phraseology of the former shows considerable variety and inventiveness. Yet it will be sufficient for our purpose to recognize that the aureate terms are as artificial as the stock phrases of the later age, and that they have as close a family resemblance among themselves. We have attempted to show that provided this elaborate diction is seen in proper perspective, and its association with the literary taste of the time is sympathetically considered, it will be found (within its own narrow limits) capable of yielding speech that is not unworthy of the name of poetry. With this in mind, let us glance at the conventional diction of the verse of some other periods in order to see if similar conclusions may be arrived at; we may thence proceed with more justification to inquire what merits are to be found in the poetic diction of the eighteenth century.

Conventional Expressions in the Ballads

The reader who has without dismay taken the leap back to the Scots Chaucerians may yet demur at a similar treatment of the Ballads, since the spirit of ballad-poetry is as different from that of most eighteenth-century verse as are the open moors from a cultivated estate, or as Sherwood Forest from the gardens of the Dukeries. Moreover, as is well known, the ballads came to be powerful dissolvents of eighteenth-century poetic complacency, and supplied the shaping impulse of some of the best lyrics of Scott, Coleridge and Wordsworth. Commenting on one of the happiest examples of Percy's partial fabrications—the conclusion of *The Heir of Lynne*—Professor Saintsbury observes 'The sweep and the rush of it are like the actual wind clearing the atmosphere. That day you read no more of the Glovers and the Masons.' Once captured by the spell, and one's return to poets of more attractive metal than the Glovers and Masons is apt to be retarded; as the return to earth of Thomas the Rhymer and other ballad-heroes was delayed through over-fond trafficking with the inhabitants of Elfland. The best ballad poetry is heady stuff; with its intensity, abruptness, and instantaneous lyricism it has the appearance of poetic experience in the raw, and this characteristic, together with its striking impersonality, has helped to favour the now declining theory of communal authorship.

In one respect, however, the ballads offer a comparison with eighteenth-century verse that is sufficiently close for our purpose, for the traditional phrases and epithets which they employ are as stereotyped and restricted in number as

the stock phrases of Augustan poets; they are not suscep-
tible of endless variation on a conventional basis, like the
aureate terms of the Scottish Chaucerians. The origin of
these phrases is connected with the origin of the ballads
themselves, and the trend of recent investigation has been
to show that the balladist put into a form suitable for oral
transmission material derived directly or indirectly from
older romances, lays, or *fabliaux*. Thus *Sir Aldingar* has been
traced back through several variants to the prose story of
William of Malmesbury, *Child Waters* is one of the many
ballads founded on the story of Griselda, and the Shetland
ballad beginning

Der lived a king inta da aste

is obscurely connected with the romance of *King Orfeo*.
Even with a ballad like *The Milldams of Binnorie*, which
besides having the semblance of originality is without any
ascertainable literary source, we cannot be sure of 'invention' on the part of the balladist, for the Shetland example
just cited has all the appearance of an indigenous and even
communal product, with its skirling music, Norse refrain,
and 'incremental repetition'; yet it is none the less an off-
shoot of a mediaeval romance. While allowing that it sometimes took up an entirely new subject, such as that of *Chevy
Chase*, we may hold with Mr. Courthope that the ballad is
'usually a *précis* of a romance'; or, if '*précis*' suggests too
deliberate a process, we may recognize that the ballad is apt
at least to absorb infiltrations from romance, in a manner
comparable to that in which the Ampleforth mummers'
play (as recently pointed out by Sir Edmund Chambers)
adapts a scene from Congreve's *Love for Love* to its own
scheme of homely pageantry. The comparison of versions
shows that the reciters of later times must be sometimes
credited with the introduction of felicitous additions and
alterations, yet it is to the conceiver and first shaper of a
ballad that the chief honours are due. Since in the majority
of instances his story was provided for him, he was free to
concentrate his abilities on casting it into a form sufficiently
condensed and vivid to capture popular enthusiasm, and on
conveying it in language both capable of being memorized
for oral transmission and of giving expression to the lyric
impulses of his audience.

We must also reckon with the fact that the social composition of the audience considerably influenced the quality of the ballad poetry. The superiority of the border poetry to the later, tamer balladry of the south has been recognized ever since Percy first made the comparison between the two. The difference may be partly accounted for on the grounds that during the later middle ages 'the people' in Scotland were more homogeneous, less split up into distinct social or professional groups than they were in England. In fifteenth-century Scotland the decay of feudalism resulted in the centralization of the cultivated school of poetry at court; the people were thus freer of imperfectly assimilated influences from polite literature, and were able to maintain a quicker and more discerning responsiveness to sung or spoken 'popular' verse. This has its bearing on the question of traditional phraseology, for though a conventional style usually accompanies an oral art (its function being to induce a receptive state of mind in the listener, as well as to facilitate memorization), with an audience of the kind for which the Lowland ballads were composed there was scope for the balladist to invest his stock phrases with an additional element of poetic suggestiveness. The conventional expressions persist, of course, in the English ballads, but they seldom have the overtones which they acquired in the north. A poet whose audience is homogeneous can employ stock phrases with more varied effect than one whose public comprises many different levels of cultural capacity. Thus the Elizabethan dramatists writing for both the court and the populace expressed themselves in adventurous, highly-figurative language, while the Restoration dramatists, addressing themselves to a small and self-contained section of society, could afford to ring the changes on a limited and formalized poetic vocabulary without fear of their diction seeming lifelessly conventional.[1] The same consideration may be held to apply, *mutatis mutandis*, to the public for whom Pope and Ambrose Philips wrote their pastorals. The art of effectively using conventional phraseology declined towards the end of the eighteenth century, just as it declined in the later ballad-poetry; and in one respect the clearing of the air which the 'natural' style of the ballads

[1]See the present writer's *Dramatic Theory and the Rhymed Heroic Play*, pp. 24–6.

helped to bring about resolves itself into a preference for a
thriving poetic diction of one type to a decadent poetic
diction of another.

In considering illustrations of the former, we will do well
to bear in mind that the ballad reaches fullest self-realization
in the form of 'lyrical tragedy'. As Professor W. P. Ker con-
clusively puts it:

> The ballads keep to their point, and that is generally a definite
> tragic problem—distress like that of *Fair Annie*, or error, as in
> *Child Maurice*, or conflict of affections or duties, as in *The
> Douglas Tragedy* or in *Bewick and Graeme*—or, in the simplest
> of them, a brave man fighting against odds, like *Johnnie of
> Braidislee*. In the more cheerful ballads, and those with a happy
> ending, like the *Gay Goss-hawk* or *Katharine Janfarie*, there is
> still the same definite sense of drama—something that has to be
> played out, rather than something that has to be continued in a
> string of adventures.[1]

The general property of the conventional phrases is to contribute to the fatalistic element which is so strong in the
ballads. In a world where sweethearts are always 'true-loves',
wine always 'bluid-red', hands always 'lily-white' and water
always 'wan', we feel that situations of a predetermined and
momentous character are likely to arise. The popularity of
the formula

> They hadna sail'd a league, a league,
> A league but barely three,

whose best-known appearance is in *Sir Patrick Spens*, but
which occurs with slight variations, such as 'ridden a mile,'
' been a week,' in several other ballads, in itself points to a
desire to stress the inevitability of the event. The bestowing
of conventional splendour on the mast and sails of a ship is
another favourite figure by means of which a tragic ending
is foreshadowed; it is to be seen at its best in *The Lass of
Lochroyan*:

> Then he's gart build a bonny ship,
> And set it on the sea,
> Wi' four-and-twenty mariners,
> To bear her company

[1] *On the History of the Ballads, 1100–1500*, Proceedings of the British Academy,
vol. IV.

> O he's gart build a bonny ship,
>   To sail on the salt sea;
> The mast was o' the beaten gold,
>   The sails o' cramoisie.[1]

The flaunting vainglory of such a vessel invites disaster, and the 'four-and-twenty mariners' have a 'fey' appearance which they would lose if they were presented in any more naturalistic manner. In *Child Waters* the conventional expressions, such as 'of *red gold* shines the gate,' and

> But my horse shall drink of the *good red wine*,
>   And you of the *water wan*

endow the hero's part of the dialogue with a timeless, universal character; they are appropriate to the recitation of an event that has the capacity to outlive historical associations and to become part of the race experience. Ellen's repetition of these set phrases, in her replies, sharpens the issue to a note of tragic endurance.

Examples bearing a general similarity to those just given are fairly numerous and need not be multiplied; sometimes, however, we meet with passages where we cannot help feeling that the balladist has imparted a more specific suggestiveness to the poetic cliché. Thus, in *Binnorie*, the conventional epithet in the lines

> She's ta'en her by the lily hand,
>   And led her down to the river-strand

conveys some of the frantic jealousy of the stronger woman at being eclipsed by the more fragile beauty of her sister. Another example of a transfigured commonplace is to be found in a particular use of the phrase 'little pen-knife.' Among the many wronged lovers, outlaws, and avenging relatives who resort to the weapon thus styled—varying in size according to the owner, but always 'little' or 'wee'— who but the King's daughter in *Glasgerion* first comes to mind when it is named?

> And then she pull'd forth a little pen-knife
>   That hangèd by her knee,
> Says, 'There shall never no churlè's blood
>   Spring within my bodye.'

[1] In *The Daemon Lover* the description of a ship with similar trappings is followed by the familiar and fatal lilt of
> 'She hadna sail'd a league, a league. . . .'

The sense of pride, the indestructible dignity of birth and rank are enhanced by the idea of her habitual wearing of this diminutive dagger. Again, in *The Douglas Tragedy*, the sense of approaching calamity, and the fiery redness of the hidden wound are stressed by their contrast to the pale diffused light which descends on the scene after the battle:

> O they rade on, and on they rade,
> And a' by the light of the moon,
> Until they came to yon wan water,
> And there they lighted down.

The device of repetition is used in the same ballad to suggest the tragic action returning on the head of the doer (thus showing unconscious conformity to 'Aristotle's best rules,' as Gray observed of *Gil Morice*); for the stanza

> He's mounted her on a milk-white steed,
> And himself on a dapple grey,
> With a bugelet horn hung down his side;
> And lightly they rode away

reappears after the fatal encounter (with its conventional imagery retained) in the following slightly altered form:

> He's lifted her on a milk-white steed,
> And himself on a dapple grey,
> With a bugelet horn hung down his side;
> And slowly they baith rade away.

It is interesting to note that the eighteenth-century collectors and editors, however much they altered and 'improved' the ballads to suit the requirements of a polished age, seldom interfered with the stock phraseology of the older poetry. Allan Ramsay, the most important ballad-editor before Percy, almost invariably touched up such genuine pieces as he included in *The Tea-Table Miscellany*. Thus *Sweet William's Ghost* (which is in substance the second part of *Clerk Saunders*, and is here printed for the first time) ends with the obviously falsified stanza:

> 'Oh stay, my own true love, stay!'
> The constant Marg'ret cried:
> Wan grew her cheeks, she clos'd her een,
> Stretch'd her soft limbs, and died.

Yet he preserves traditional ballad expressions which occur earlier in the poem, such as 'her lily-white hand,' and

> Now she has kilted her robes of green
> A piece below her knee.

As for the *Reliques*, it is probable that Percy would have patched his material less freely had he not submitted to Shenstone's guidance during the preparation of the work. Shenstone's letter (of February 3, 1762) to Percy, who had recently been staying with him in order to discuss editorial problems, sufficiently shows the attitude of the former:

> . . . if you publish these old pieces *unimproved* only, I consider them as not everyone's money, but as a prize merely for either virtuosoes, or else the manufacturers in this kind of ware: the Poets namely. . . . If you consider *improved* copies as the *standard* or *principal* ones, and give them a first place, I do not see that you need hereby violate your purpose of arranging according to the date. They may still rank as old Barons, let the robes they wear be ever so modern.

Shenstone died in February 1764, a year before the *Reliques* were published, and during the interval Percy may have felt freer to limit his renovations, in a few selected ballads such as *Child Waters* and *Glasgerion*, to slight verbal changes. Shenstone's pseudo-ballad, *Jemmy Dawson*, chiefly remembered for its unfortunate line

> Oh, Dawson, monarch of my heart

may have been included in the *Reliques* partly by way of reparation. As it is, Percy's alterations, though generally distasteful to modern readers familiar with the received versions, are decidedly less so than those of the later ballad-editor Pinkerton, who lacked the excuse of having to gain the public ear. The inappropriate happy ending tacked on to *The Child of Elle* shows the most indefensible aspect of Percy's editing; it will be noticed, however, in the first of two stanzas which may be quoted from it, that he introduces a traditional phrase as if to add flavour to an otherwise characterless piece of verse.

> Here take her, Child of Elle, he sayd,
> And gave her lillye hand;
> Here take my deare and only child,
> And with her half my land:

> Thy father once mine honour wrongde
> In dayes of youthful pride;
> Do thou the injurye repayre
> In fondnesse for thy bride.

Similarly, the expression 'true-love' appears in the ending which Percy more successfully (as Wordsworth observed) bestowed on *Sir Cauline*, and 'the good red gold' gleams in the concluding verses which he wrote for *The Heir of Lynne*. He preserves 'the bluid-red wine' in *Spens* and the 'little pen-knife' in *Glasgerion*. Thomas Evans, too, retains the set phrases in his collection of *Old Ballads* (4 volumes, 1784), though his alterations are slight compared with those of most ballad editors of the century. The most valuable part of his work consists in the inclusion of many Robin Hood ballads that had hitherto escaped the collector's net; and in these he faithfully preserves conventional elements, such as

> Then Robin set his back against a tree,
> And his foot against a thorn

—the traditional attitude taken in preparing for some resolute action. In the version which he gives of *Johnny Armstrang's Last Goodnight*, we find

> A cowardly Scot came from behind,
> And run him through the fair bodye.

Here the first line has been slightly retouched, but the second, with its stock phrase, is preserved intact.

If their work points in many ways to a transitional state of taste, it can hardly be said that the eighteenth-century ballad editors were conscious of preparing the way for a grand revolution in poetic aims. They did not hold that the taste for the polished verse of their contemporaries was likely to be dispelled by the appeal of these more roughly-moulded treasures of the past. It does not seem unjustifiable to suppose, therefore, that their evident appreciation of the formal elements in the oral poetry—or, as Percy put it, 'a cast of style and measure very different from that of contemporary poets of a higher class; [and] many phrases and idioms, which the minstrels seem to have appropriated to themselves'—may have been quickened by the fact that an equally conventional phraseology was prevalent in the verse of their own age.

Virgil and his Translators; Dryden and Warton

It is fairly well recognized that the origin of many of the conventional phrases used by eighteenth-century poets is to be found in Latin poetry, particularly that of Virgil. So considerable was the influence of Virgil on the nature-poetry of the period that we may discern two widely-practised and recurrent types of verse—the pastoral and the didactic—whose sources are clearly to be found in the *Eclogues* or the *Georgics* of the Latin poet. It will be seen, too, that many of the writers may be grouped according to whether the prevailing tendency of their nature-poetry is idyllic, or practical and purposive; we have on the one hand the artificers of pastorals such as Pope, Gay, Ambrose Philips, Shenstone and Cunningham, and on the other the authors of 'judicious precepts' such as Dyer, Grainger, Smart, Somerville and Armstrong. In both types of poem we are apt to encounter passages where Virgil has been openly imitated; thus in Shenstone's *Pastoral Ballad* the lines

> I have found out a gift for my fair;
> I have found where the wood-pigeons breed

are merely a happy rendering of a passage in Virgil's third *Eclogue:*

> Parta meae Veneri sunt munera; namque notavi
> ipse locum, aëriae quo congessere palumbes.

Parts of *The Seasons* are indebted to the Georgics for their shaping idea, and Thomson sometimes paraphrases Virgil's lines for the purpose of filling out his own periods. The description of the approaching storm in *Winter*, for instance, depends on the first *Georgic* for much of its imagery; thus

> With broadened nostrils to the sky upturned
> The conscious heifer snuffs the stormy gale

is drawn from

> ... bucula caelum
> suspiciens patulis captavit naribus auras

while in the account of the storm at sea the familiar phrase fluctusque ad sidera tollit' is expanded into

> . . . the mountain billows to the clouds
> In dreadful tumult swelled.

But in order to compare the Latin with the English manner of using set poetic expressions, we can hardly do better than pick out some examples of the latter in Virgil and then find what the neo-classic translators have made of them. As might be expected, however, the inquiry will more frequently suggest itself as to what justification there may be for the use of stock phrases in the translation where none are to be found in the original. A theoretical defence of this practice may be derived from the views of the neo-classic translators themselves. Denham and Waller, who are usually credited with instituting the school of regular coupletry in English verse may be held to have wrought a similar change in the method of translating from the classics. In their renderings of portions of Virgil both cultivated a freer manner in dealing with the text than had obtained during the previous age, and Denham in an essay which accompanied his version (published in 1656) defended the innovation by declaring 'I conceive it to be a vulgar error, in translating poets, to affect being a *fidus interpres* . . . if Virgil must needs speak English, it were fit he should speak not only as a man of this Nation, but as a man of this Age.'

Among 'the mob of gentlemen who wrote with ease' there were few who did not try their skill at turning an *Eclogue* or a *Georgic* into smooth distichs, yet though this activity continued after the appearance of Dryden's version, his remained the standard translation of Virgil during the eighteenth century, as Pope's continued to be that of Homer. Dryden's version, as is generally recognized, was written negligently and in haste, yet it is arguable that whatever pains he bestowed on it he would have been incapable of reproducing the spirit and style of Virgil's finest passages, whereas the confident swing and energy of his unhampered style give the work an indestructible individuality which it would otherwise have probably lacked. The liberties, if not the inaccuracies of his translation stand excusable in the light of his avowed aim, which is set forth in the *Dedication of the Aeneid*:

Lay by Virgil . . . when you take my version . . . . The way I have taken is not so straight as metaphrase, nor so loose as paraphrase: some things too I have omitted, and sometimes have added of my own. . . . I have endeavoured to make Virgil speak such English as he would himself have spoken, if he had been born in England, and in this present age.

It will be seen that this is in complete accord with Denham's view of translation, and though both statements seem to show an indifference to the special merits of Virgil's style, the intention to avoid Latinisms is more apparent than real. Neither do these principles conflict with that other typically neo-classic pronouncement of Gray's, 'the language of the age is never the language of poetry,' for Denham and Dryden do not refer to colloquial idiom but to the literary language. The aim of the neo-classic translators was, in a sense, to render Virgil in a more classical language than that of the original. The pseudo-classic diction—both the lofty Miltonic kind in which Latinism of construction and wealth of vocabulary predominated, and the Dryden-Pope type in which set-phrases and *gradus* epithets were variously combined—was such a florid elaboration of its Latin proto-types that it became no longer a Latin diction, and acquired instead a capacity for artistic embellishment suitable to the special requirements of English verse; much as in the sphere of plastic art, applied ornament derived from classical sources achieved a notable individuality in the work of the Adam brothers. Eighteenth-century poetic diction has its classical flavour and associations, but these are for the most part indirect; as a literary artifice, therefore, it should be judged on its own merits in performance and not as a derivative practice, not as Latinity run to seed.

It is necessary to keep this consideration in mind when encountering parallel Latin and English set phrases; some of which may now be cited from Virgil and his translators. We may regard it as significant that Latin conventional poetic expressions are apt to diverge (if not so extensively as their English counterparts) from the language of normal usage. A good instance is to be seen in the use of the epithet *purpureus*, whose meaning was extended in poetry to include not only the colour purple and its related hues, but also the ideas of brightness and beauty. Dryden in using the phrase 'purple daffodils' was not translating literally from Virgil, who in the passage in question merely has 'narcisso floreat alnus,'[1] but he gave the word its acquired Latin meaning in order to heighten his style in a striking manner.

Virgil's stock phrases may be broadly divided into those whose affinities are with the pastoral, and those whose purpose it is to lend dignity to the epic style. Exactly parallel word-combinations in English verse derive more frequently from the former than from the latter class. Thus in the *Eclogues* we find *liquidi fontes*, the origin of the familiar 'liquid fountains' whose use was widespread until the reaction against Pope set in. Among the pre-romantic opponents of stereotyped diction there were some who made bold to question Virgil's taste in this direction; thus Hugh Blair in his *Lectures on Rhetoric* (published 1783) took the uncompromising view that no generalized descriptions were tolerable in poetry, and maintained that Virgil's *liquidi fontes* must be assigned to the class of phrases where epithets are brought in merely 'to complete the verse, or make the rhyme answer . . . expletive words only, which in place of adding anything to the description, clog and enervate it . . . for to denote by an epithet that water is liquid or that snow is white, is no better than mere tautology.' It is hardly necessary to defend Virgil on this score, for it is evident that he used such phrases (which occur far less frequently in the *Eclogues* than in the translations or original pastorals of eighteenth-century writers) not out of a poverty of descriptive vocabulary but of set purpose, as being conducive to the pastoral atmosphere of agreeable semi-unreality.

Dryden's version of a landscape passage in the first book of the *Aeneid* provides an interesting comparison with the original:

> a *sylvan scene*
> Appears above, and groves for ever green:
> A grot is formed beneath, with mossy seats,
> To rest the Nereids, and exclude the heats.
> Down through the crannies of the living walls,
> The *crystal streams* descend in *murmuring falls.*

[1]Eighth *Eclogue.* Cf. the description of the heroine's dress in a Swedish version of the Hero and Leander ballad as 'the scarlet white, likewise the scarlet blue' (cited by Gummere, *The Popular Ballad*).

Virgil's picture is executed in fewer, and surer strokes:

> tum *silvis scaena* coruscis
> desuper, horrentique atrum nemus imminet umbra;
> fronte sub adversa scopulis pendentibus antrum,
> intus aquae dulces vivoque sedilia saxo,
> Nympharum domus.[1]

Here we may consider it fitting that Virgil should confine himself to general properties and large appearances, for the prominent features of the scene are all that would be likely to strike the mariners forced to put in at an unknown African harbour, but it will be noticed that Dryden readily takes the opportunity to introduce three stock phrases in his translation where one sufficed in the Latin. The same proportion in the number of stock phrases employed by translator and poet may be observed in Joseph Warton's rendering of a passage in the tenth *Eclogue*. Virgil's conciseness seems appropriate to the sharper outlines of Italian scenery:

> mecum inter salices lenta sub vite iaceret;
> serta mihi Phyllis legeret, cantaret Amyntas.
> hic *gelidi fontes*, hic mollia prata, Lycori,
> hic nemus; hic ipso tecum consumerer aevo.[2]

Warton's diffuseness, on the other hand, seems more suited to an English landscape of lush pastures and swelling woodlands:

> There as we lay the vine's thick shades beneath,
> The boy should sing, and Phillis twine the wreath.
> Here *cooling fountains* roll thro' *flow'ry meads*,
> Here woods, Lycoris! Lift their *verdant heads*,
> Here could I wear my careless life away,
> And in thy arms insensibly decay.

Here the abundance of stock phrases may cause the more surprise as coming from the man who helped to break down the tyranny of the school of artificial coupletry, and who in his dislike of abstract terms in poetry went so far as to complain that 'even Virgil himself is not free from this fault, but is frequently general and undiscriminating, where Homer is minutely circumstantial.' In the Prefatory Dedica-

[1] I, 164–8.   [2] *Ecl.* x, 40–4.

tion (1753) to his translated edition[1] Warton regrets that for
the purpose of nature-description 'a set of hereditary objects
has been continued from one poet to another, which have
been often made use of without any propriety either as to
age or climate.' That he particularly disapproved of the
practice is shown by his repetition of the charge with additional emphasis three years later, in his *Essay on the Genius
and Writings of Pope*: 'Hence that nauseous repetition of the
same circumstances; hence that disgusting impropriety of
introducing what may be called a set of hereditary images,
without proper regard to the age, or climate, or occasion in
which they were formerly used.' Yet in the same essay
Warton quotes as an example of 'exactness of description'
the passage from Thomson's *Summer* which opens

> Around the adjoining brook that *purls* along
> The *vocal grove*

and whose effect may be said to depend on the skill with
which familiar or stereotyped words are conjoined with
more vivid images. It is hardly probable that Warton wished
to rule out every manifestation of what we should call stock
diction, for in speaking of the style to be adopted in translating the *Eclogues*, he observes

> It requires no small command of language, to be able to carry
> on Pastoral Dialogues, without sinking into vulgar idioms, to
> unite simplicity with grace, and to preserve familiarity without
> flatness. A style too highly elevated would be nauseously un-
> natural, and one too prosaic and plebeian, would be insipid and
> unaffecting. . . . And perhaps it may be observed in general, that
> if the Romans ever excelled their Grecian masters in the graces
> of diction, it was owing to their exerting all their powers, in
> dressing up those thoughts and ideas that were ready found to
> their hands.

He sees, therefore, in Virgil's *Eclogues* a discerning and
sensitive use of ornamental poetic language, but is aware
that in attempting to reproduce the grace and dignity of the
Latin there is a danger of losing its freshness and precision.
If the following extracts are compared with the original, it
will be seen that he has approached the via media far more

[1]*The Works of Virgil in English Verse*, 4 vols., Dodsley, 1763. The Aeneid translated by the Rev. Mr. Christopher Pitt; the Eclogues and Georgics, with notes on
the whole, by the Rev. Mr. Joseph Warton.

nearly than Dryden, whose version seems to show no perception of the immediacy and truth of the sequestered scene
as portrayed by Virgil in the well-known lines:

> fortunate senex, hic inter flumina nota
> et fontis sacros frigus captabis opacum.
> hinc tibi, quae semper, vicino ab limite saepes
> Hyblaeis apibus florem depasta salicti
> saepe levi somnum suadebit inire susurro;
> hinc alta sub rupe canet frondator ad auras:
> nec tamen interea raucae, tua cura, palumbes,
> nec gemere aeria cessabit turtur ab ulmo.

There is something in the very sound of these lines that
suggests an Italian landscape; there is an unchanging firm-
ness of outlines in the unsubdued light, and the rock rises
more boldly and abruptly than in either of the English
versions, while the blended cooings of the wood-pigeons and
turtle-doves appear to have been for long ages past associated
with the scene. Dryden's rendering is as follows:

> Behold! yon bordering fence of sallow-trees
> Is fraught with flowers; the flowers are fraught with bees;
> The busy bees, with a soft murmuring strain,
> Invite to gentle sleep the labouring swain.
> While from the neighbouring rock, with rural songs,
> The pruner's voice the pleasing dream prolongs,
> Stock-doves and turtles tell their amorous pain,
> And, from the lofty elms, of love complain.

Here the stock diction falsifies the nuances of Virgil's
descriptive language; thus the suggestion of strangeness and
beauty in the snatches of the woodman's song is frigidly
glazed over by the hackneyed phrase 'with rural songs,'
while the familiar poetic 'property' associated with turtles—
'amorous pain'—is a poor substitute for the caressing mur-
mur and verbal magic of Virgil's last line. Dryden's translation is freer than Warton's (which is quoted below) but the
difference in manner may be attributed to carelessness
rather than to an attempt to communicate in an individual
way the spirit and atmosphere of the original.

> Happy old man! here 'mid the custom'd streams
> And sacred springs, you'll shun the scorching beams,
> While from yon willow-fence, thy pasture's bound,
> The bees that suck their flowery stores around,

> Shall sweetly mingle, with the whispering boughs,
> Their lulling murmurs, and invite repose:
> While from steep rocks the pruner's song is heard;
> Nor the soft-cooing dove, thy fav'rite bird,
> Mean while shall cease to breathe her melting strain,
> Nor turtles from th' aërial elm to plain.

Warton's rendering is two lines longer than Dryden's, and suffers somewhat owing to this diffusion; we should consider it as a good verse paraphrase rather than as a masterly reproduction of a poem in a different medium. But the stereotyped phrases, such as 'scorching beams' and 'flowery stores,' do not obscure felicities in the original as they do in Dryden's version, the pruner's song fares better at Warton's hands, while he has endeavoured to recapture, and not unsuccessfully, the undulation of vowel-sounds in the final line.

The style of the *Georgics* differs from that of the *Eclogues* in many ways, one of the most prominent being the smaller number of stock phrases employed therein. Yet in their translations of the *Georgics* neither Dryden nor Warton show much attempt to chasten their poetic diction in this respect. For one of Virgil's charming incidental pictures, in the fourth *Georgic:*

> hoc geritur Zephyris primum impellentibus undas,
> ante novis rubeant quam prata coloribus, ante
> garrula quam tignis nidum suspendat hirundo

Dryden has

> This must be done ere spring makes equal day,
> When western winds on curling waters play;
> Ere painted meads produce their flowery crops,
> Or swallows twitter on the chimney tops.

Trochaic epithets are equally plentiful in Warton's version, but his 'crimson' is at least a nearer approach to the Latin than Dryden's 'painted,' and he avoids the effect of flabby periphrasis and secures some suggestion of pictorial continuity by simply substituting 'ere' for Dryden's 'or' in the last line.

> Be this perform'd when Zephyr's balmy breeze
> First curls the surface of the smiling seas,
> Ere bloom the meads in crimson vesture drest,
> Ere swallows twitter o'er the new-built nest.

Warton's observations on the style of the *Georgics* are to be found in his *Reflections on Didactic Poetry,* an essay appended to his translation of the works. He borrows several phrases from Addison's *Essay on Virgil's Georgics,* and in general adopts his view that the manner must be consistently elevated in order to atone for the prosaic and technical character of the precepts conveyed.

> But as the didactic poet speaks in his own person, it is necessary and proper for him to use a more luscious colouring of style, and to be more studious of ornament. . . . Accordingly, Virgil hath used every possible method of exalting his style into dignity and grace, by bold metaphors, Grecisms, striking epithets, and poetical circumlocutions.

It is noteworthy that the stock phraseology proliferates far more freely in the couplet translations of the *Georgics* than in the blank verse didactic-descriptive poems of the period; and indeed the latter (influenced in varying degrees by Milton, Thomson and Virgil) often approach nearer to the style, if not the spirit, of the *Georgics* than the translations themselves. The allusive and learned manner, the use of sonorous proper names, the similes and poetical digressions which abound in them, all have their forerunners in the Latin poem. It is hardly necessary to provide illustrations of these embellishments in the *Georgics,* but a single example may be quoted, in connection with which it may be recalled that Addison found it a matter for admiration that Virgil 'delivers the meanest of his precepts with a kind of grandeur, he breaks the clods and tosses the dung about with an air of gracefulness':

> Multum adeo, rastris glaebas qui frangit inertis
> vimineasque trahit crates, iuvat arva, neque illum
> flava Ceres alto nequiquam spectat Olympo.[1]

This passage may have been particularly in his mind when he wrote, but it is to be observed that the last line, though defensible purely on the score of interspersing the succession of precepts with colour and variety, has the additional advantage (seldom seen in eighteenth-century productions of the kind) of conveying a sense of the kindly spirit of earth befriending and helping the husbandman as he works. It

[1] I, 94–6.

has not the character of a frigid importation of mythological statuary.

The Latinism of construction which is so marked a feature of eighteenth-century blank verse descriptive poems —the unusual syntactic order, the free inversions, sandwiched nouns and double negatives—may be attributed to the influence of Virgil at least as much as to that of any other classical poet, though the manner of adopting these forms in English verse is almost invariably based on the example of Milton. To take but one instance—that of the double negatives; their frequent appearance in *The Seasons* (e.g. 'Nor is the night unwished') may have derived from the practice of Philips:

> Nor are the hills unamiable. . . .
>
> *Cyder* I, 563.

or from the example of Milton:

> Nor was his eare less peal'd
> With noises loud and ruinous (to compare
> Great things with small) than when Bellona storms
>
> *P.L.* II, 920–2.

or from their ultimate source in the poetry of the classics, from which we may quote the following Virgilian instance:

> Nec tamen, haec cum sint hominumque boumque labores
> versando terram experti, nihil improbus anser
> Strymoniaeque grues et amaris intiba fibris
> officiunt aut umbra nocet
>
> *Georgics* I, 118–21.

We have remarked that eighteenth-century diction shows resemblances to Virgil's epic, as well as his bucolic style. Here we are more concerned with a recognizable type of heightening than with stock phraseology, although Virgil has recurrent epic phrases (after the manner of Homer) such as 'in medias acies,' 'mirabile dictu,' 'sub pectore vulnus' and the like. Occasionally these are borrowed in English verse, as can be seen in the quotation above from Milton, with its adoption of the Virgilian 'si parva licet componere magnis.' In the eighteenth century, however, the serious epic was rarely attempted, the spirit of the age was hostile to its growth, and the few that were produced, such as Glover's

Leonidas, show all the vices of laboured pompousness that are usually associated with the pseudo-classic style. Lofty phraseology of an epic cast is seen to best advantage in the blank-verse descriptive pieces devoted to practical and rural themes; it is also used in satirical mock-heroic poems such as the *Dunciad, Scribleriad* and *Rosciad.* The former type of poem, which alone need concern us, has too often been summarily condemned in this respect, for although it undoubtedly shows an over-partiality for circuitous pedantries of expression, the fastening of elevated descriptive language on to everyday objects frequently results in felicitous effects; the practice, moreover, has the sanction of notable examples in Virgil and Milton. The most conspicuous instance in Virgil of this activity (and perhaps the source of all its later manifestations) is to be found in his playfully pompous account of the bee communities in the fourth *Georgic.* Here the poet treats the vicissitudes of insect life with a gentle, almost tender irony. He delights in the free and apparently irresponsible application of his epic vocabulary to a homely theme, and shows considerable art in heightening his language to the point where it becomes rotund without swelling into an entirely burlesque style.

> praeterea regem non sic Aegyptus et ingens
> Lydia nec populi Parthorum aut Medus Hydaspes
> observant.

In view of the influence which this manner of writing exerted over the didactic-descriptive poems of the age, it will be well to compare a representative passage from the fourth Georgic with its renderings by our two translators. Let us take the account of the battle between the rival hosts of bees, a passage which Virgil plentifully besprinkles with heroic expressions:—

> Sin autem ad pugnam exierint—nam saepe duobus
> regibus incessit magno discordia motu;
> continuoque animos volgi et trepidantia bello
> corda licet longe praesciscere; namque morantis
> Martius ille aeris rauci canor increpat et vox
> auditur fractos sonitus imitata tubarum;
> tum trepidae inter se coeunt, pennisque coruscant
> spiculaque exacuunt rostris aptantque lacertos

et circa regem atque ipsa ad praetoria densae
miscentur magnisque vocant clamoribus hostem:

· · · ·

Ipsi per medias acies insignibus alis
ingentis animos angusto in pectore versant,
usque adeo obnixi non cedere, dum gravis aut hos
aut hos versa fuga victor dare terga subnegit.
Hi motus animorum atque haec certamina tanta
pulveris exigui iactu compressa quiescunt.

It is hardly necessary to draw attention to the praiseworthy
manner in which the prolonged loftiness and mounting
ardour of this description are interrupted by the laconic
decisiveness of the last line. The freedom of Dryden's
translation shows to advantage here: and we can see that the
author of the triumphant mock-heroic, *MacFlecknoe*, and of so
many flamboyant heroic plays has no difficulty in recapturing the ironic grandiosity of the original. The happy exuberance of the added line

Inflamed with ire, and trembling with disdain

is in itself enough to show how Dryden gains through not
adhering closely to the Latin.

But, if intestine broils alarm the hive
(For two pretenders oft for empire strive),
The vulgar in divided factions jar;
And murmuring sounds proclaim the civil war.
Inflamed with ire, and trembling with disdain,
Scarce can their limbs their mighty souls contain.
With shouts, the coward's courage they excite,
And martial clangours call them out to fight:
With hoarse alarms the hollow camp rebounds,
That imitate the trumpet's angry sounds.

· · · ·

Full in the midst the haughty monarchs ride;
The trusty guards come up, and close the side;
With shouts the daring foe to battle is defied.
With mighty souls in narrow bodies prest,
They challenge, and encounter breast to breast;
So fixed on fame, unknowing how to fly
And obstinately bent to win or die
That long the doubtful combat they maintain,
Till one prevails—for only one can reign.
Yet all these dreadful deeds, this deadly fray,

A cast of scattered dust will soon allay,
And undecided leave the fortune of the day.

Warton, though he makes use of the language of heroics in
his version, is far less spirited than Dryden, and is more
preoccupied with faithfully translating his author than with
communicating the precise shade of extravagance on which
the effect of the passage depends. Almost the only license
he allows himself is the introduction of the epithet 'lagging'
in the tenth line.

> But if intent on war they seek the foe,
> 'Twixt two contending kings when discords glow,
> The peoples' troubled minds you soon presage,
> Burning for battle, swoln with eager rage;
> Hark! a rough clangor calls the hosts to arms!
> A voice, like the deep trumpet's hoarse alarms!
> Furious they meet, and brandishing their wings,
> Fit all their claws, and sharpen all their stings;
> Around their monarch's high pavilion crowd,
> And call the lagging foe with shoutings loud.
>
> .   .   .   .   .
>
> The Kings shine glorious 'mid the thickest war,
> And mighty souls in narrow bosoms bear:
> Steadfast in fight, unknowing how to yield,
> Till these or those forsake the deathful field.
> These fierce contentions, this pernicious fray,
> A little dust flung upwards will allay.

Almost equally striking is Dryden's success in fancifully
expanding the lines

> tum corpora luce carentum
> exportant tectis et tristia funera ducunt[1]

into

> And crowds of dead, that never must return
> To their loved hives, in decent pomp are borne:
> Their friends attend the hearse; the next relations mourn.

Here Warton merely has

> Forth the dead citizens with grief are borne,
> In solemn state the sad attendants mourn.

The quotations we have given will be sufficient to show
that examples were not wanting, either in Virgil or in the
translators, of an imaginative playfulness well suited to the

[1] IV, 255–6.

classically-influenced poets of the seventeenth and eighteenth centuries who wished to impart lightness and variety to their verse without forfeiting the distinction of the epic style. As may be frequently seen in eighteenth-century poetry, it was only by a fairly close adherence to the conventions of a set diction that such nuances were obtainable. Happy effects of the kind are often discoverable in works of a monumental aspect, like tufts of grass and flowers in the crevices of a classical façade. Milton, with his 'tame villatic fowl,' Thomson with a decisive touch like

> The stork-assembly meets; for many a day
> Consulting deep and various

Cowper drawing from his rich resources of language a phrase like 'twisted form vermicular'; the authors of phrases of this type not only show a connoisseur's relish in the amenities of a settled style; they illuminate the object from a fresh angle by revealing its unconscious humour. The gradations between parody, mimicry, and poetry written in a borrowed style are often imperceptible. Who can decide where the first of these ends and the last begins, in Shenstone's *Schoolmistress*? Much of Lamb's prose reproduces the mannerisms of the seventeenth-century masters, but his adoption of their peculiarities and oddities of expression served to release the springs of his own creative gift. It is doubtful whether Cowper would have flowed so freely if he had not allowed himself frequent depredations on the conventional expressions of poets of the previous age, and the same may be said even of Wordsworth, especially the youthful Wordsworth of *An Evening Walk* and the *Descriptive Sketches*.

It behoves us therefore to treat both the rotund expressions and the stock phrases of eighteenth-century nature poets with somewhat more indulgence than they commonly receive, and to be prepared occasionally to encounter subtle and suggestive descriptive touches contrived by means of them. We have seen poetic effects won from an apt use of conventional phraseology in the poetry of the Scottish Chaucerians, in the Ballads, and finally in Virgil, and with these examples in mind, should be able to approach the diction of eighteenth-century verse the more open-mindedly.

As to the translations we have been considering, it is easy enough to point to the stucco-like plastering of stereotyped expressions on to Virgil as typical of the artificiality of the age, but here we would do well to recall Johnson's pronouncement: 'We must try its effect as an English poem; that is the way to judge of the merit of a translation. Translations are, in general, for people who cannot read the original.' Arbitrary in some respects though this may be as an independent critical assertion, it succinctly shows what most of the neo-classic translators were aiming at. They had a confidence in the potentialities of pseudo-classic diction; a quality that reappears in the work of the better poets of the period, and there invites our discriminating attention.

CHAPTER III

THEORIES OF GENERALIZED FORM AND DICTION IN CRITICISM OF THE CLASSICAL PERIOD

TO what extent, we may ask, do neo-classic critics discriminate between the imaginative and the mechanical use of artificial descriptive phrases in poetry? It must be admitted that clearly-made distinctions of this sort are not common. On the other hand we frequently meet with general statements as to the characteristics of a style appropriate for a particular purpose, from which a nicety of choice in the employment of stock phrases may be inferred; such as in Pope's advertisement to his *Pastorals*:

> . . . the manners not too polite nor too rustic; the thoughts are plain, yet admit a little quickness and passion, but that short and flowing; the expression humble, yet as pure as the language will afford; neat, but not florid; easy, and yet lively.

The comparative scarcity of direct statements on the subject may be partly attributed to the fact that during the earlier half of the century critics were, on the whole, more interested in the gradual perfecting of the mechanism of the Popian and neo-Miltonic styles than in the judicious and sensitive application of them.

> Tho' still some traces of our rustic vein
> And splay-foot verse, remain'd, and will remain.

Thus Addison censured Milton (who, rather than Dryden, is now recognized as the ultimate source of 'poetic diction') for not being consistently Miltonic in *Paradise Lost*. In taking exception to such phrases as 'No fear lest dinner cool' and 'For this we may thank Adam' on account of their colloquial character, Addison showed an undue attention to the outward characteristics of the grand style, and an inability to perceive the additional strength that these idiomatic contrasts imparted to the texture of the verse. Yet Milton had himself given an indication, in one of his prose pamphlets, of the value of such contrasts:

> Doth not Christ himself teach the highest things by the similitude of old bottles and patched clothes? Doth he not illus-

trate best things by things most evil—His own coming to be as a thief in the night, and the righteous man's wisdom to that of an unjust steward?[1]

The principle was recognized by Pope, in his Postscript to the *Odyssey* (and later by Joseph Warton, in his *Reflections on Didactic Poetry*):

> The imitators of Milton ... are a hundred times more obsolete and cramp than he, and equally so in all places: Whereas it should have been observed of Milton that he is not lavish of his exotick words and phrases everywhere alike, but employs them much more where the subject is marvellous, vast and strange, as in the scenes of Heaven, Hell, Chaos, etc. than where it is turn'd to the natural and agreeable, as in the pictures of Paradise, the loves of our first parents, the entertainments of Angels, and the like.

and it was borne out in practice, if less frequently than we should wish, by Thomson in *The Seasons*.[2]

There is hardly a literary topic discussed by Dryden on which he did not change his mind at least once in the course of his critical career, and his treatment of the rival claims of detailed and generalized description provides a good example of his vigorous empiricism. The repudiation of technical terms in poetry, occasioned by his reflections on the style to be adopted in translating the *Aeneid*, might seem to denote a loss in freshness and power in comparison with his exuberant use of them in his early poem *Annus Mirabilis*, but there is little doubt that Johnson was right in questioning the effectiveness of the mallet and the calking-iron in that piece. Nor does Dryden, the translator not only of the *Aeneid*, but also of the *Georgics*, advocate vagueness of expression when he asserts that Virgil 'writ not to mariners, soldiers, astronomers, gardeners, peasants, etc., but to all in general and in particular men and ladies of the first

---

[1] *An Apology against a Pamphlet called A Modest Confutation.*
[2] For a good example of his simpler and more direct style, cf. his picture of the winter robin:

> Half-afraid he first
> Against the window beats; then brisk alights
> On the warm hearth; then, hopping o'er the floor,
> Eyes all the smiling family askance,
> And pecks, and starts, and wonders where he is;
> Till, more familiar grown, the table-crumbs
> Attract his slender feet.
>
> *Winter*, 250–6.

quality, who have been better bred than to be too nicely knowing in the terms.' His range of vision has extended, he is less intent on the parts than on the whole. The principle underlying much of the cult of 'general properties and large appearances' was one of composition; whether as applied to the plan of a whole work, or to the grouping of the parts of a landscape, or, more subtly, to the distribution and effective interplay of stereotyped or Latinized descriptive phrases. Hence many of the better kind of neo-classic pronouncements on order, harmony, and balance should be considered also in their bearings on the question of a discriminating use of poetic diction, and *vice versa*. The following passage from *A Parallel of Poetry and Painting* though its subject is design and arrangement, is as applicable to 'generalized description' as to 'generalized form':

> They [poetry and painting] present us with images more perfect than the life in any individual; and we have the pleasure to see all the scattered beauties of nature united by a happy chemistry, without its deformities or faults.

While in illustration of the opposite characteristic, a quotation from the *Dedication of the Aeneis* will serve to show that the poet who considered 'set wide the palace gates' preferable to 'unlock the door,' and who used such phrases as 'the loquacious race' for frogs, and 'the frugal kind' for bees, was more likely to be aiming at a total poetic effect than at empty adornment:

> I will not excuse, but justify myself, for one pretended crime, with which I am liable to be charged by false critics, not only in this translation, but in many of my original poems: that I Latinize too much. 'Tis true that, when I find an English word significant and sounding, I neither borrow from the Latin nor any other language; but, when I want at home, I must seek abroad; . . . Poetry requires ornament; and that is not to be had from our old Teuton monosyllables . . . [But] a poet must first be certain that the word he would introduce is beautiful in the Latin, and is to consider, in the next place, whether it will agree with the English idiom; after this, he ought to take the opinion of judicious friends, such as are learned in both languages: and, lastly, since no man is infallible, let him use this license very sparingly.

Pope distinguishes clearly enough in the *Essay on Criticism* between set phrases used in a lifeless manner and those manipulated in such a way as to convey some distinctness of impression.

> Where-e'er you find 'the cooling western breeze,'
> In the next line, it 'whispers through the trees':
> If crystal streams 'with pleasing murmurs creep,'
> The reader's threaten'd (not in vain) with 'sleep':
> . . . True ease in writing comes from art, not chance,
> As those move easiest who have learn'd to dance.
> 'Tis not enough no harshness gives offence,
> The sound must seem an echo to the sense:
> Soft is the strain when Zephyr gently blows,
> And the smooth stream in smoother numbers flows;
> But when loud surges lash the sounding shore,
> The hoarse, rough verse should like the torrent roar:

It is true that he is dealing primarily with 'numbers,' and is concerned with discarding vapid smoothness in favour of onomatopoeic skill, but the principle of 'animated correctness,' as we may call it, is none the less introduced. The rejection of lifeless ornamental phrases on the part of one who has been generally credited with their invention is in any case striking, and brings to mind his own comparison between the genuine and the neo-Miltonic styles. The Popian dialect, in the derogatory sense, was similarly less the product of Pope himself than of his imitators; the latter were apt to employ the ornate splendour of the Homer translation on themes no more ambitious in scope than *Windsor Forest*, whose descriptive language, as will be later shown, actually displays an almost perfect adaptation of means to ends.

In Johnson's criticism, there are several instances of spurious ornament condemned, but hardly any indications that he appreciated the suggestive potentiality of stock phrases. The doctrine of 'general properties and large appearances' had with him more reference to the form and thought-content than to the sensuous side of poetry, whereas it is largely by their skilfully-contrived appeal to the senses that the best eighteenth-century set-phrase descriptions need to be estimated. Johnson's defects of eye have been exaggerated; in his later life his receptiveness towards natural beauty increased, and the delight in the sense of recognition which *The Seasons* afforded him ought not to cause surprise when his frequently expressed admiration for the scenery of Scotland and Wales, during his tours in those countries, is taken into account. But his deafness, though not so impenetrable as to prevent a few of the harmonies of Milton's blank verse from filtering through, was yet enough of a barrier to withhold from him some of the clearest strains of Pope's lyre.

I have been told that the couplet by which he declared his own ear to be most gratified, was this:

Lo, where Maeotis sleeps, and hardly flows
The freezing Tanais through a waste of snows

But the reason of this preference I cannot discover.

In his opinion, Pope had brought the art of 'numbers' to its highest pitch of perfection, yet if he was capable of missing the musical suggestiveness of lines like these, it is hardly likely that he would have been able to appreciate the less obvious musical values obtained by Pope's conjunctions of conventional phrases. On the other hand failure to discern merits does not involve inability to detect blemishes, and this is especially true of Johnson, who however staunch an advocate of a 'system of words at once refined from the grossness of domestick use, and free from the harshness of terms appropriated to particular arts,' nevertheless could not tolerate some of the empty rotundities of Thomson's poetic language, and showed an equal impatience with the otiose ornamental epithets that occur in Pope's *Homer*. The uniform smoothness of the couplet was often promoted by the introduction of a trochaic epithet before the final word in a line, and Johnson observing that these epithets tend to be artificial and superfluous, aptly pointed out that by losing two syllables apiece the first six lines of Pope's *Iliad* could be converted into octosyllabic couplets with little loss of meaning.

It is not easy to place Goldsmith as a critic—indeed he is usually denied the rank of one—owing to the waywardness and eccentricity of his individual judgements. But the reasons which he gives for admiring certain styles in poetry throw some light on his own peculiarly individual manner of versification, one in which the *gradus* epithets are used sparingly, and seldom without good reason for their presence. He shares Johnson's distrust of the poetic innovations of the day, and together they fight an Augustan rearguard action, though without planned co-operation, against ode-writers, mediaevalists, Spenserian imitators, mythologists, and all who without unusually good cause depart from the standard of correctness set up by Dryden, Addison and Pope. 'These misguided innovators,' says Goldsmith, in his *Life of Parnell*, 'have not been content with restoring antiquated words and phrases, but have indulged themselves in the most licentious transpositions and the harshest constructions, vainly imagining, that the more their writings are unlike prose, the more they resemble poetry.' That this is in accord with Johnson's view of the matter is shown by the fact that the latter borrows the concluding statement of the passage for the purpose of censuring the irregularity of Collins' lyrics. But Goldsmith lacks Johnson's faculty of rising superior to his own prejudices in the presence of work of unquestionable power; thus, unlike Johnson he allows his aversion for blank verse (most stridently expressed in the Dedication of *The Traveller*) to obscure from him the qualities of Thomson, whom he considers 'a verbose and affected poet.' In his best poem, *The Deserted Village*, Goldsmith's style is perfectly suited to the matter expressed; simple and direct enough to permit the convincing reproduction of rural scenes and characters, yet capable of spreading an agreeable golden haze over the whole—in which a line like

> No cheerful murmurs fluctuate in the gale

with its conventional elements, does not in the least strike as inappropriate. There would however seem to be a considerable inconsistency between the happy mingling of the precise and the general in his own expression and the tenor of his remarks on the styles of other poets. He disapproves, for instance, of 'Ay, there's the rub' as being 'a vulgarism beneath the dignity of Hamlet's character,' and in his essay *On Poetry as distinguished from other writing* he approves of Pope's embellishing the simplicity of Homer:

> For example, the Grecian bard says simply, the sun rose; and his translator gives us a beautiful picture of the sun rising. Homer mentions a person who played upon the lyre; the translator sets him before us warbling to the silver strings. If this be a deviation, it is at the same time an improvement.

Poetry by this process would become in effect, what he calls it, 'a species of painting with words'; a misconception of aim which Lessing with his insistence on the beauty of Homer's economy of epithets, was doing his best to rectify in his contemporarily written *Laokoon*. But against this we may set his pronouncement on Parnell whom he contrasts with the 'misguided innovators,' and whose best work shows a knowledge of when to use and when to refrain from the ornamental set phrase:

> He has considered the language of poetry as the language of life, and conveys the warmest thoughts in the simplest expression.

In eighteenth-century writing, the particular is apt to lie concealed in the general, and from Goldsmith's scattered remarks on the virtue of 'composition' in poetry we may often infer that awareness of the necessity for a skilful choice of imagery which we know to have been his in practice.

> It is the business of art [and also of poetry] to imitate nature, but not with a servile pencil: and to choose those attitudes and dispositions only, which are beautiful and engaging. . . . To copy nature is a task the most bungling workman is able to execute; to select such parts as contribute to delight, is reserved only for those whom accident has blest with uncommon talents. . . .

Among the desultory remarks on diction that Gray lets fall in the course of his too scanty criticism the most important is the well-known observation in his letter to West (of April, 1742) that 'the language of the age is never the language of poetry.' The correspondence that called forth this remark had to do with the dramatic fitness of the style which Gray adopted for his (fragmentary) tragedy *Aggripina*, to which West had justly taken exception on account of its over-indulgence in Shakespearian reminiscences. Conscious, probably, of the felicities attainable in other realms of poetry besides drama by his favourite method of exquisitely careful poetic inlay, Gray in self-justification points to the four major poets' practice of enriching the language with foreign idioms, archaisms and new-coined words. His dictum therefore applies to poetic diction in its broadest sense, and not chiefly (as is sometimes supposed) to the types in vogue in the eighteenth century. In order to see how far Gray approved of the contemporary stock phraseology for pur-

poses of nature-description we have to turn to his own poems
which, coming from so conscious a craftsman, have an
almost critical validity in themselves.

It is not without significance that in his early group of
poems, written in the same year as the letter to West,
Gray almost invariably uses the accepted Popian diction for
depicting nature. Since his effects are carefully premeditated
these poetic clichés are generally attuned to the predominant
sentiment of the poem. Thus in the *Ode on the Spring*, which
is not a poem of lyrical impulse in the accepted sense, but a
semi-humorous 'moral' meditation, phrases such as 'the
purple year,' 'the Attic warbler,' 'the panting herds' are in
keeping with the general air of designed elegance, while they
convey at the same time enough of the sensuous enjoyment of
a spring day to conduce towards a unity of impression.
Similarly some tincture of classical language would seem to
be inevitable in a mood of lofty musing on an august theme
like '*A Distant Prospect of Eton College*'—a corresponding
tendency is to be seen, under the spell of a prospect of
Oxford, in Arnold's *Thyrsis*—and the 'gales,' the 'watry
glade,' and 'margent green' have a deliberate and almost
sanctified indistinctness which plays its part in the total
effect. But Gray's chief weakness is also apparent in the
poem, and the multiplication of 'horrid' personifications
in the seventh and eighth stanzas cannot fail to jar on
readers of a later day. The only other poem of the early
group that concerns us here is the *Sonnet on the Death of
Richard West*. There is no doubt that Wordsworth was well-
advised in choosing this piece to illustrate the mutual
antagonism of the pure and the ornate styles, and it is noteworthy that the condemned portion of the sonnet consists
entirely of nature-description. Stilted expressions such as:

> And redning Phoebus lifts his golden fire

call to mind Gray's later strictures on Lyttelton's *Monody*
to the memory of his wife: 'poetical ornaments are foreign
to the purpose; for they only show a man is not sorry.' Had
the background of nature been conceived more vividly
the poignancy of contrast might have been more successfully conveyed. The stock phraseology need not have been
avoided, but by this means it would have taken on some
suggestion of animation.

Gray's later poems show that while the depiction of nature in terms of Popian diction is still retained, his descriptive resources are greatly enlarged, even to the point of an occasional use of 'the language of the age.' Thus in the *Elegy* (written mainly between 1746 and 1750) the phrase 'the lowing herd' is drawn from the stock diction, though owing to the impression of gradually decreasing distinctness which the first stanza conveys, the fact is readily overlooked. The context similarly redeems the 'nodding beech' (l. 101) from any suggestion of lifeless artificiality, though the same cannot be said of the apparently irresistible abstractions 'Fair Science,' 'Melancholy' and the like which help to render the Epitaph redundant. On the other hand we have also a combination of descriptive expressions drawn from a variety of sources; for instance, a line of pure poetry such as

> And drowsy tinklings lull the distant folds—

which is diction in the sense that it is distinct from the ordinary language of men, but manifesting a kind of perfection that is peculiarly Gray's; a line like

> Save where the beetle wheels his droning flight

which is probably indebted to Collins's *Ode to Evening*; and, as an example of 'the language of the age'

> 'the swallow twitt'ring from the straw-built shed'

which though it could not be said more simply, or more vividly, is by virtue of its position as perfectly subdued to the general composition as are the better-placed stock phrases remarked on above. *The Bard* has touches of nature-description, though owing to its Pindaric character the simple and unadorned style is appropriately absent. The conventional language attains a certain splendour in the familiar passage:

> Fair laughs the Morn, and soft the Zephyr blows
> While proudly riding o'er the azure realm
> In gallant trim the gilded Vessel goes
> Youth on the prow, and Pleasure at the helm;

Coleridge took exception to the concluding line on the grounds that it depended 'wholly on the compositors putting or not putting a small Capital, both in this and in many other passages of the same poet, whether the words should be personifications or mere abstractions.' While the reproof is

just enough with regard to Gray's general practice, it seems
to be unnecessarily harsh as applied to the present quotation,
where the effect aimed at is one of sumptuous if superficial
allegory, somewhat in the style of an Italian wall-painting
of the High Renaissance. The wild and stormy setting of
the poem—'On a rock, whose haughty brow, 'etc.—is swiftly
and convincingly portrayed in a style of diction derived
from Milton, as Gray's note confirms, but completely
individualized in the process of borrowing.

No better examples are to be found in Gray's poetry of
nature depicted with the utmost simplicity and truth than in
the unfinished *Ode on the Pleasure Arising from Vicissitude*:

> The meanest flowret of the vale
> The simplest note that swells the gale
> The common sun, the air, the skies,
> To him are opening Paradise.

Here the touch is almost Wordsworthian, though there is
also, in the string of personified abstractions which precedes
the passage, evidence of the 'curiously elaborate' style
which Wordsworth deprecated. In the opening lines of the
ode, however, we are given personification of an entirely
different order:

> Now the golden Morn aloft
> Waves her dew-bespangled wing;
> With vermeil cheek and whisper soft
> She woo's the tardy spring.

This has, in addition to a kind of Elizabethan opulence that
is pleasing in itself, the vital faculty of encouraging the
imagination to paint the appropriate scene in its own forms
and colours, a quality sadly absent from the greater number
of Gray's personifications, which are either too thin or too
rigidly outlined to contribute anything of poetic value to
their surroundings.

The mixture of pomposity and perfections in this piece is
characteristic of nearly all Gray's poetry. But apart from one
or two exceptions, such as the unsightly 'nodding groves'
in *The Progress of Poesy*, Gray's 'cumbrous splendour' is
not due to an inability to distinguish between the felicitous
and the mechanical use of the stock phrase, for as has been
incidentally shown, he was unusually discerning in this

respect. It may be attributed, rather, to his strain of scholarly dilettantism (most clearly revealed in the correspondence with Walpole), which led him to experiment with high-sounding phrases in the hopes of enriching still further his already composite style.

Perhaps the most comprehensive treatment in eighteenth-century English literature of the principles underlying the doctrine of generalized form is to be found in Sir Joshua Reynolds's fifteen *Discourses* (1769–90). The breadth of view which he so often displays, and his discerning admiration for successful departures from a central standard of excellence, are circumstances of more critical importance than the fact that his artistic beliefs would theoretically discountenance many later developments of poetry and painting. It was however chiefly for the latter reason that he was assailed by nineteenth-century critics such as Hazlitt and Ruskin, who evincing the Romantic hostility towards 'rules,' and to any theory which tended to direct nature into a preconceived pattern, sought to invalidate Reynolds's principles by displaying his 'inconsistencies' of judgement. Hazlitt, it must be owned, showed more agility of pen than soundness of judgement on this subject. It is true that a statement of Reynolds such as 'the whole beauty and grandeur of the art consists, in my opinion, in being able to get above all singular forms, local customs, particularities, and details of every kind' appears to warrant Hazlitt's general objection that such a theory would 'blend them [the varied manifestations of nature] into a vague, vapid, nondescript *ideal* conception, which pretends to unite but, in reality destroys. Sir Joshua's theory limits nature and paralyses art.' But it must be remembered that Reynolds is primarily concerned with fostering an admiration for the 'Grand Style,' which in painting, as in the epic, undoubtedly includes among its important characteristics the faculty of transcending the particular without evaporating into vagueness.

Showing similar symptoms of alarm lest such precepts should arbitrarily limit the scope of the artist and hamper his invention, Ruskin takes exception to Reynolds's statement in the *Idler* concerning Michelangelo and Homer that 'In painting, as in poetry, the highest style has the

least of common nature,' and points out that Homer describes cookery, shows a wife's sorrow at parting from her
husband, and a child's fright at its father's helmet. Yet
Reynolds in his well-known exposition of the 'point of
repose' as one of the characteristics of great art[1] had himself
drawn attention to the fact that Homer 'from the midst of
battles and horrors, relieves and refreshes the mind of the
reader, by introducing some quiet rural image, or picture of
familiar domestic life.' This is the type of remark that Hazlitt
chooses to brandish about before adding it to his collection
of Reynolds's 'inconsistencies.' But while much hasty
judgement may be excused to those who were privileged to
share the *emportement* of the Romantic cause, the fact remains that most of Reynolds's alleged inconsistencies were
in reality qualifications; the necessary and wise qualifications
of a critic who seeking to disseminate a faculty for recognizing the highest art and the understanding of its principles,
was yet too vividly aware of the happy diversity of lower
but legitimate styles, and of the endless variety of nature, to
rest content in mere dogmatism. On the other hand in view
of his statement that 'The excellence of portrait-painting
. . . depends more upon the general effect produced by the
painter, than on the exact expression of the peculiarities, or
minute discrimination of the parts,' there are some grounds
for Ruskin's comment on the gap between Reynolds's theory
and his practice:

> . . . he enforced with his lips generalization and idealism, while
> with his pencil he was tracing the patterns of the dresses of the
> belles of his day; he exhorted his pupils to attend only to the
> invariable, while he himself was occupied in distinguishing every
> variation of womanly temper.

Reynolds's fortunate partiality for the copious and luxuriant
in his own portraits may be associated with his relish of
these qualities in the work of the Venetian painters; for the
more he deprecates the introduction of sensuous splendour
by these painters into works of an elevated character, the
more it is evident that he has been captivated by their
exciting glow and warmth from the purely pictorial point of
view. It should moreover be remembered that he wrote at a

[1] *Eighth Discourse.*

time when the taste of the age was in a state of transition, when dignity had to compete with strangeness and irregularity, and admiration for his own window at New College chapel vied (in Warton's poem) with enthusiasm for its Gothic setting.

But these considerations do not diminish the positive value of his main theories. His direct observations on poetry are few, and are less important in themselves than as showing his belief that the same broad principles applied to both arts. Thus he contends that just as the highest type of painting rises above a bare imitation of nature, so poetry confesses a similar aim in its adoption of metre and of a language removed from ordinary speech; just as a skilfully-composed landscape is superior to an 'ordinary view,' so Milton's *L'Allegro* and *Il Penseroso* by their masterly selection and arrangement of natural objects have more suggestive value than 'a cold prosaic narration or description.' A brief reference to some of his further views on the nature of 'generalized form,' particularly with regard to landscape painting, may therefore throw some light from a fresh angle on the technique and aims of the classicizing nature-poets of his age.

First should be noticed the frequency with which he reiterates the caution that an idealized subject does not connote vagueness of treatment. Two statements may be profitably compared; the first concerning the grand style of painting, with its standards drawn from the practice of Raphael and Michelangelo :

> I should be sorry, if what is here recommended, should be at all understood to countenance a careless or indetermined manner of painting. For though the painter is to overlook the accidental discriminations of nature, he is to exhibit distinctly, and with precision, the general forms of things. . . . he who possesses the knowledge of the exact form which every part of nature ought to have, will be fond of expressing that knowledge with correctness and precision in all his works.[1]

The second brings up the same point in connection with landscape-painting, in whose domain the palm, in Reynolds's view, goes to Claude on account of his masterly power of

[1]*Third Discourse.*

combining separate scenes of nature into one idealized whole:

> But whether landscape painting has a right to aspire so far as to reject what the painters call accidents of nature, is not easy to determine. It is certain Claude Lorrain seldom, if ever, availed himself of those accidents; either he thought that such peculiarities were contrary to that style of general nature which he professed, or that it would catch the attention too strongly, and destroy that quietness and repose which he thought necessary to that kind of painting.[1]

In the loftier style, the ability to portray the particular, though not directly revealed, has its effect in the depiction of the general, whereas in landscape although the avoidance of literalism is triumphantly justified in the practice of Claude, the question is commendably left open. Reynolds's suspension of judgement with reference to a style of landscape which he was inclined to prefer may be contrasted with Ruskin's violent partisanship, on behalf of Turner, against the 'dim, stupid, serene, leguminous enjoyment of Claude's sunny afternoon.'

Transferred to the field of nature-poetry, an analogous judgement to that contained in the second quotation would be one which fully valued the skilful composition and concealed or subordinated particularity of Pope's *Pastorals* and *Windsor Forest*, but recognized the rival claims of the freely detailed descriptive method apparent in *The Seasons*. The lively interest in both the Dutch and the Italian schools of landscape on the part of eighteenth-century English poets is sufficiently well attested to make it probable that the latter derived suggestions from their favourite artists for the formation of a set descriptive method, and Reynolds's judgement may in his own day have been recognizably as applicable to landscape poetry as to landscape painting. Among his various remarks on landscape painting, that kind deserves to be most stressed which advocates detailed observation and the ability to depict objects with precision as a necessary condition of the power to generalize successfully:

> A landscape-painter certainly ought to study anatomically (if I may use the expression) all the objects which he paints; but

[1] *Fourth Discourse.*

when he is to turn his studies to use, his skill, as a man of genius, will be displayed in showing the general effect, preserving the same degree of hardness and softness which the objects have in nature.[1]

A recognition of the probability that the same principle animated several of the descriptions of nature in Popian language will profitably put us on our guard against the standardized verdicts on these pieces which are apt to appear in the manuals of literature, and help us to appraise the 'feign'd neglect' with which their authors 'sunk partial form in general effect.'

[1]*Eleventh Discourse*. Cf. Lessing's comment in *Laokoon* XVII, after quoting from a confusedly detailed 'botanist's' poem: 'I only ask him what is the case with respect to the conception of the whole? If this also is to be vivid, no individual prominence must be given to single parts.'

PART TWO

CHAPTER IV

'PICTORIAL' DESCRIPTION AND LANDSCAPE ART

AMONG the obstacles in the way of a proper appreciation of eighteenth-century nature poetry perhaps the most formidable next to (and partly associated with) the aversion for poetic diction is the theory that in it description is too often regarded as an end in itself. It is generally recognized that after the appearance of *The Seasons* the type of poem in which nature was used mainly as a decorative background for the social activities of man gave way to a kind of poem in which lengthy and more detailed descriptions of chosen scenes provided the chief opportunity for the exercise of the poetic talent, and it is commonly assumed that whereas this development marked a progress in consciousness and prepared the way for the Romantic poets, the verse itself is too lacking either in emotional intensity or in a sense of the 'cosmic' to achieve much in the way of absolute value. The following may be taken as fairly representative of the kind of assertion prevalent in literary histories:

> In the study of the evolution of the love of Nature from Waller to Wordsworth . . . the second stage is marked by the recognition of the world about us as beautiful and worthy of close study, but this study is detailed and external rather than penetrating and suggestive. Very much work of the transition period is of this sort.[1]

While such verdicts do not in themselves discourage a renewed scrutiny of the main stretches and by-ways of pre-romantic nature poetry, they tend to the conclusion that the historical estimate is all that may be expected from such inquiries. Without going so far as some who in the fashionable wave of anti-romanticism have played with the notion that Wordsworth wrote of nature less perceptively when he forsook pure description and sought for 'a remoter charm by thought supplied,' it may still be held that the

[1] Myra Reynolds, *The Treatment of Nature in English Poetry Between Pope and Wordsworth*. Chicago, 1909. pp. 27-8.

nature poem of the eighteenth century differs from its Romantic counterpart in kind rather than in degree, and requires to be judged by its own standards. In the older style of poetry the personal viewpoint of the poet though not unimportant is not essential, as it is to the Romantic nature poem. The depiction of rural sights and occupations is apt to be leisurely, intimate, and desultory, suggesting a conviction that such an intercourse with nature is beneficent in itself and does not require a deliberate evocation of the higher modes of thought and feeling in order to justify the activity. It is a mistake to assume that the placidity of this poetry necessarily betokens shallowness. The verse of the Thomson school especially, is pervaded by a wholesome, semi-pagan, natural piety; it is more often implied than expressed, and the concealment usually results in poetic gain, but when it is explicit it takes the form of a pantheistic sense of communion with nature, as in *The Seasons* themselves. In so far as poetry that has these characteristics can be charged with 'regarding description as an end in itself,' the eighteenth century may be cheerfully convicted of a copiousness of production in this vein that has been hardly rivalled in later times.

Within recent years, however, an important study has appeared, some of whose bearings unless carefully examined would give strong support from a new quarter to the notion that the nature-poetry of the period was factitious in aim and external in treatment. In the preface to her *Italian Landscape in Eighteenth Century England*[1], Miss E. W. Manwaring states that 'the landscape which was taken as a model by Thomson and Dyer, by Kent and Shenstone, by Mrs. Radcliffe, was Italian, the landscape of the seventeenth-century painters, Claude, Salvator, the Poussins, and the long line of their followers and imitators, French, Dutch and English.' This writer collects an enormous mass of evidence to show how widespread was the vogue for Claude and Salvator among the cultivated world of the day and how it manifested itself in the activities of the collectors and painters both amateur and professional, the travellers, landscape-gardeners, novelists, and finally the poets. Mr. C. Hussey in *The Picturesque* (1927) has followed in her wake,

[1]New York, 1925.

distinguishing however the later picturesque style (with its
greater variety and irregularity) from the 'ideal' (or purely
Claudian-Salvatorial), and discovering its presence in a
multitude of different forms, varying from Reynolds's
Discourses to London street architecture. Thomson and
Dyer are taken as representative landscape poets and are
discussed in some detail. So far as it is possible to summarize
his somewhat inconsistent views on these writers, it may be
said that he considers that Thomson though unaffected by
any particular painter, unmistakably showed the influence
of the art-gallery or print portfolio in his manner of composing his descriptions; while Dyer whose sense of formal
composition was defective—except, it is curiously alleged,
in *Grongar Hill* itself[1] consciously strove to reproduce the
effects of landscape artists, especially those of Claude, in
his poetry.

But the specialized study of 'influences' on poetry is
notoriously apt to lead to the pitfall of supposing that extensive borrowing in itself results in verse that is artificial and
derivative. Miss Manwaring (in particular) does not alto-
gether avoid this fallacy and appears to think that its effects
may pass unnoticed by adopting the traditional patronizing
attitude towards eighteenth-century poetry. Her method of
marshalling all the passages of verse that show a resemblance
to the landscapes of Claude and Salvator is misleading, since
it encourages the notion that the poets aimed at Italianizing
English landscape.   Similarly as regards the painters and
engravers. Her subject constrains her to devote her attention
to the artists who were *most* indebted to Claude and Salvator,
while the best of them, such as J. R. Cozens, Girtin,
Towne, and Cotman, she practically ignores. Yet the poets
whose work we are estimating have far more correspondences
both in technique and angle of vision with these painters,
than they have with Claude, Salvator, Gaspar, and their
imitators.

Leaving aside for the moment the actual examples of
poetic indebtedness to the two Italian masters, let us consider
the inferences drawn from this survey. Firstly, it is contended that owing to excessive admiration for these painters,
landscape art was regarded in a regrettably literary manner

[1]Cf. *infra*, p. 101.

and there resulted 'a confusion of standards and weakness of taste which classed the feeble imitation with the great original, and partly accounts for the monstrosities which developed in the landscape gardening, and the general monotony of the conceptions of landscape beauty.' Here we may note that the impression of monotony is generally caused by the imaginative failure of the reader, familiar with the wider range of nineteenth-century nature-poetry, to secure the precise focus that will reveal the many nuances of tone and colour within the more conventional style. Moreover, Miss Manwaring considers that the 'feeble imitation' of nature at second hand was in accordance with a prevalent pseudo-Aristotelian doctrine of idealization, one which was given concise expression by Thomas Twining when in a dissertation (1789) on the Poetics he approved of 'those models of *improved and selected nature*, which it is the business of the landscape painter to exhibit.' We have seen, however, from Reynolds's *Discourses* that idealized form in landscape was not held to exclude either detailed description or first-hand observation of nature; it was the necessity for an expressive design that was salutarily kept uppermost in such theories.

Secondly, since on these considerations the bulk of eighteenth-century nature-poetry is found to be essentially artificial, it is valued not for its achievement but for its preparation of the ground for later and richer growths:

> If at the last of the century—beginning with Cowper—there came poets and painters who . . . found beauty in hedge-rows and cornfields, and in Hampstead and Mousehold Heaths, it was because of a long training in seeing landscape pictorially—a training which of necessity began with the most elaborate and heightened forms of landscape, with the richest and most obvious appeal, and on the vast and impressive scale.

Realism, however, is only one of the characteristics of romanticism, and is not essential to it. The fact that Claude and Salvator also kindled the imaginations of Wordsworth, Keats and Hazlitt (as Miss Manwaring herself notes) should warn us against distrusting the association between poetry and landscape painting. Wordsworth could combine delicate truth to nature with idealization in his poetry, and it is notable that in his Essay of 1815, he subordinates the

merit of the 'eye on the object' to that of the feelings of the
poet urging him 'to work upon it [the object] in the spirit of
genuine imagination.' He also clearly implies that first
hand description of nature was more in evidence in the period
intervening between Thomson and his own day, than in that
between Pope and Thomson. Indeed we might deduce from
Wordsworth that there is nothing inherently wrong about
the generalized style; only that it must, like all other styles,
conform to the poetic requirement of 'imaginative truth.'

It will be recalled that 'seeing landscape pictorially' was
one of the chief manifestations of false poetic taste which
Lessing set out to counteract in the *Laokoon*.

> To enumerate one by one to the reader, in order to afford him
> an idea of the whole, several parts of things, which, if they are to
> produce a whole I must necessarily in nature take in at one glance,
> is an encroachment by the poet upon the sphere of the painter, whereby
> he squanders much imagination to no purpose.

If Miss Manwaring's conclusions are accepted, then
Lessing's case against eighteenth-century descriptive poetry
would appear to be substantiated beyond question. Yet it is
curious that he never gives examples of actual imitation in
poetry of the landscape style of a particular artist or school
of painters. Are we to conclude then that he was unaware of
the immense vogue of connoisseurship in landscape art
which prevailed during his own time, and which, we are
invited to believe, caused the very poets whose style he
deprecated to fashion their descriptive method on that of
the two most widely known and easily recognizable landscape masters? It is more probable that such instances of
imitation as he may have noticed were to him of slight
importance compared to the general distinctions which he
wished to make clear. Lessing was a philosophical critic of
a high order, and knew how to keep the study of 'influences'
in its proper place. His tendency is to argue like Coleridge
from one illuminating principle to the next and to confine
himself to the most cogent illustrations only. In fact, no
more satisfactory exposure of the delusiveness of the
'influences' in question could be wished for than that which
Lessing himself provides:

> If, however, the poet and the artist cannot help frequently
> contemplating those objects, which are common to both, from

the same point of view, it must happen that in many cases their imitations harmonize, without the least copying or rivalry between the two having taken place. These coincidences between contemporaneous artists and poets . . . may lead to mutual illustration. But to push this kind of illustration to such refinements that coincidence is converted into design; and to impute to the poet, especially in every trifle, a reference to this statue, or that painting, is to render him a very doubtful service; and not him alone, but the reader also, to whom the most beautiful passages are by these means rendered, if you will, very significant, but at the same time terribly cold.

And it must be admitted that by these means Miss Manwaring sometimes makes the winter of our presumed discontent with eighteenth-century poetry unnecessarily glacial. As for Lessing, his case against descriptive poetry deserves to be judged separately, and on its own merits; to attempt to support his conclusions with others drawn from poetic examples that have not been judged on their merits is to confuse the issue.

To return, then, to the question of the effect of Claude and Salvator on the nature-poets; it may in general be maintained that there is no harm in a poet being taught to look at nature in a particular way, or for particular effects, by a painter, provided he produces a satisfying re-creation in the terms of his own art. That the poets' appreciation of the English countryside was enhanced by their admiration for Claudian distances and Salvatorial glooms is, after all, only what might be expected; and from this point of view the light thrown on the poetry by the paintings is of value in helping us to recapture the focus and angle of vision of these nature-enthusiasts. The very fact that their field of vision was circumscribed (in comparison with that of the Romantics and their successors) enabled them to dwell with keener pleasure on certain harmonies of colour and sound, certain groupings of light and shade and mass, and to present certain scenes with more relish than we are capable of nowadays. The mutual illustration of the two arts helps us in the not easy task of seeing the world through their eyes and of appraising some of their easily overlooked felicities.

In turning our attention to such similarities as appear between the artists and the poets, two facts should be borne in mind.   In the first place the enthusiasm for landscape art preceded by a good many years the first attempts of the poets to turn to nature in search of new subject-matter. Pictures, prints and drawings collected by gentlemen on their travels were flowing fast into England during the opening years of the century, whereas it was not until the first decade had passed that the renewal of interest in nature begins to show itself, in the poetry of Lady Winchilsea and Parnell. Secondly, it is known that many of the poets were either keenly interested in or themselves practised the art of landscape-painting. Thus Gray and Scott of Amwell were active connoisseurs, while Shenstone and Dyer were amateur artists. Dyer indeed started with the intention of making art his profession, but finding the life precarious took orders in order to be able to marry.   He studied under the critic-artist Jonathan Richardson who, as is shown in his *Theory of Painting* (1715), was an ardent devotee of Claude and Salvator, and no doubt familiarized his pupil with their work. It is probable that Dyer came even more under the sway of these painters when he went to Rome in order to complete his art-studies, and in his poem *The Ruins of Rome* one passage at least shows an intention to convey a Claudian effect:

> . . . the rising sun
> Flames on the ruins in the purer air
> Towering aloft, upon the glittering plain,
> Like broken rocks, a vast circumference;
> Rent palaces, crushed columns, rifted moles,
> Fanes rolled on fanes, and tombs on buried tombs.

In this, many of the Claudian elements are present, such as the extensive plain with its amphitheatre form and the variegated classic ruins bathed in a sunrise glow, but the indebtedness to the painter may be held to be at least more excusable here, owing to the identity of subject-matter, than it would have been had Dyer tried to describe his Cambrian hills in a similar manner.

Grongar Hill, however, does not escape Miss Manwaring's detective vigilance, for though she recognizes that it is 'not composed in one single picture,' she holds that it 'presents Claude's wide country outspread, rivers, woods, and hills,' and in illustration of such word-painting, quotes the lines:

> Old castles on the cliffs arise,
> Proudly towering in the skies!
> Rushing from the woods, the spires
> Seem from hence ascending fires!
> Half his beams Apollo sheds
> On the yellow mountain-heads!
> Gilds the fleeces of the flocks:
> And glitters on the broken rocks!

But if Claudian influence may be attributed to any similar depiction of an extensive dawn or sunset view, we might proceed to make kindred quotations from the poets indefinitely; or in the same manner we might maintain that in the passage which includes the lines:

> And there the poisonous adder breeds,
> Concealed in ruins, moss and weeds,
> While, ever and anon, there falls
> Huge heaps of hoary mouldered walls

Dyer was emulating Salvator's treatment of wild scenery and desolate ruins. That Dyer has here successfully transmuted into poetry all traces of his merely pictorial bent is suggested by the fact that later in the century, critics accustomed to the more elaborate groupings of scenic visions prevalent among the disciples of Thomson censured Dyer for not composing in the same vein. Thus, the Rev. William Gilpin, an inveterate champion of the 'correctly picturesque,' who considered that three cows would compose well in a view but not two, complains in his *Observations on the River Wye* that in *Grongar Hill* there is no clear contrast between foreground and distance—'His hill's extensive view would probably have afforded several completed landscapes, but it is not clear that he aimed at producing any.' Had he done so, however, his poetry would have been more exposed to Lessing's general charges than it is. But Dyer is essentially a describer of 'prospects' rather than of landscapes. The distinction between the two was well expressed by Shenstone: 'I use the words landskip or prospect, the former as expressive of home scenes, the latter of distant images. Prospects should take in the blue distant hills; but never so remotely, that they are not distinguishable from clouds[1] . . . Landskip

---

[1] In Shenstone's essay on *The Hermit*, the character thus entitled preferred 'a well-discriminated landskip' to 'a distant and promiscuous azure.'

should contain variety enough to form a picture upon
canvas.' A further treatment of this point may be reserved
until we discuss Dyer's method of descriptive composition,
together with that of other nature-poets.

Precision of outline is less a characteristic of Claude
than of Salvator, and this being so we might expect that in
his more conventional style with its preference for generic
terms Pope would give us many reminiscences of Claudian
scenes. Yet the fact that among all his descriptive passages
only two can be said to have any clear affinities with this
style of landscape may cause us to doubt whether Pope
owed his quickening impulse to Claude as much as to his
own observation, and especially to his love of the surroundings amidst which he was brought up. The following lines
from the *Temple of Fame*, however, readily bring to the eye
one of Claude's elaborate harbour-pieces:

> Here sailing ships delight the wandering eyes;
> There trees, and intermingled temples rise:
> Now a clear sun the shining scene displays;
> The transient landscape now in clouds decays.

In the other example, from *Windsor Forest*, the inappropri-
ateness of the second line suggests that the poet's eye was
for the moment more on imaginary Claudian distances than
on the slight undulations of the domain in question:

> Here in full light the russet plains extend:
> There wrapp'd in clouds the blueish hills ascend.

To what extent James Thomson was familiar with the art
of Claude and Salvator during the period in which he was
writing the first version of *The Seasons* is a matter of conjecture so far as the external evidence goes. The Countess of
Hertford, one of his patrons, was a lover of pictures and an
amateur artist. The painter Aikman was one of his friends,
and had spent three years in Italy. From the oft quoted
passage in *The Castle of Indolence* which gives first a Salvatorial and then a Claudian sketch:

> Now the black tempest strikes the astonished eyes;
> Now down the steep the flashing torrent flies;
> The trembling sun now plays o'er ocean blue,
> And now rude mountains frown amid the skies:

and ends with the lines:

Whate'er Lorraine light-touched with softening hue,
Or savage Rosa dashed, or learned Poussin drew.

it seems clear that he was predisposed to admire the work of these artists, though since *The Seasons* was published before and the *Castle of Indolence* was written after his own visit to Italy, it is probable that his enthusiasm for painting was more pronounced during his later years. In his essay on Pope, Joseph Warton noticed that 'The scenes of Thomson are frequently as wild and romantic as those of Salvator Rosa, pleasingly varied with precipices and torrents, and "castled cliffs," and deep vallies, with piny mountains, and the gloomiest caverns.' His object, of course, was to make an apt comparison, not to suggest that Thomson had tried to imitate the painter. *The Seasons*, and *Summer* in particular contain many examples of such scenes, but it is seldom possible to determine whether memories of the valley of the Jedwater and Teviotdale, flashes of suggestion from Salvator, or pure inventiveness predominates in them. The only element in such descriptions which may be considered as specifically Salvatorial is the presence of dead or blasted trees of fantastic form; a good instance occurs in the account of the storm in mountainous country:

> Black from the stroke, above, the smouldering pine
> Stands a sad shattered trunk; and, stretched below
> A lifeless group the blasted cattle lie.[1]

But Thomson comes nearest to Salvator in a passage from *Liberty*, which was written after his visit to Italy, and where he is describing not nature, but landscape-painting:

> . . . the precipice frowned, dire;
> White, down the rock, the rushing torrent dashed;
> The sun shone, trembling, o'er the distant main;
> The tempest foamed, immense; the driving storm
> Saddened the skies, and, from the doubling gloom,
> On the scathed oak the ragged lightning fell . . .

Like those reminiscent of Salvator, scenes which have a general resemblance to Claude's pictures occur most plentifully in *Summer*. The following is a typical instance:

[1] *Summer* 1150–3. The description of the waterfall in *Summer* 590–606 perhaps owes something to Salvator, but it may equally well have been suggested by a landscape of Gaspar Poussin, who specialized in cascades.

But yonder comes the powerful king of day, . . .
He looks in boundless majesty abroad;
And sheds the shining day, that burnished plays
On rocks, and hills, and towers, and wandering streams,
High-gleaming from afar.

While there is nothing in such an example to suggest imitation of or rivalry with a Claudian view, it is quite possible that in thus depicting a sunrise in general terms the poet may have been unconsciously influenced by an aggregate of memories drawn from the artist's work. In *Spring*, Miss Manwaring discovers only two passages that are indebted to Italian painting. One is the masterly picture of rapid sunlight after vernal showers, which in its movement and glittering vitality seems to be quite foreign to Claude and to presage, rather, Constable's larger and more ambitious landscape style:

The rapid radiance instantaneous strikes
The illumined mountain, through the forest streams,
Shakes on the floods, and in a yellow mist,
Far smoking o'er the interminable plain,
In twinkling myriads lights the dewy gems.
Moist, bright, and green, the landscape laughs around.

The other is the famous description of the view from Hagley Park:

Meantime, you gain the Height, from whose fair Brow
The bursting Prospect spreads immense around . . . *etc.*

This, written 'after his visit to Italy and his collecting of prints,' is alleged to be 'the most elaborately composed of all his landscapes, with real Claudian distances.' But one of the most notable features of the description seems to be that owing to the vast extent of the view and multiplicity of the objects taken in, it is not a formal composition at all. It is what Thomson names it, a 'prospect,' and as such it may be reserved for later comment, together with Dyer's technique in this type of depiction. We may remark here, however, that the passage was in all probability written at Hagley Park itself, for Thomson spent a good part of the year 1743 at his friend Lyttelton's estate on the task of improving and enlarging his poem, and the paragraph which contains the lines in question first appeared in the edition of 1744.

There would seem to be some grounds, therefore, for supposing that the description shows more exactitude of impression than the Claudian idealization to which a memory-picture might lend itself.

But if Thomson was as ready as has been alleged to depict views in a Claudian manner which favoured such treatment, we should naturally expect to find a poetic landscape of this kind in the accompanying description of the grounds of Hagley Park. For these had been laid out for Lyttelton as a *ferme ornée* after the designs of William Kent, the popularizer of the serpentine and the ha-ha, and the originator of the style which since it was founded on landscape-painting, came to be known as landscape-gardening. Kent owed something to Salvator, but was chiefly influenced by Claude, as can be seen from his fondness for winding waters and concave declivities surrounded by groves, and especially from the profusion of temples which adorn the grounds of Stowe, his most elaborate undertaking. Horace Walpole, too, associates Hagley with Claude in his *Essay on Gardening* (1771). The lines in question are addressed to Lyttelton:

> There, along the dale,
> With woods o'erhung, and shagged with mossy rocks,
> Whence on each hand the gushing waters play,
> And down the rough cascade white-dashing fall,
> Or gleam in lengthened vista through the trees,
> You silent steal; or sit beneath the shade
> Of solemn oaks, that tuft the swelling mounts
> Thrown graceful round by nature's careless hand,
> And pensive listen to the various voice
> Of rural peace: the herds, the flocks, the birds,
> The hollow-whispering breeze, the plaint of rills,
> That, purling down amid the twisted roots
> Which creep around, their dewy murmurs shake
> On the soothed ear.

But there is nothing here that suggests Claude, and no mention is made of the distinctively Claudian 'objects' of the estate; the Attic temple and Sanderson Miller's specially-constructed ruin. Nor, unless we happened to be aware, from such sources as Walpole's correspondence and Smith of Derby's attractively spacious picture, that the grounds were adorned with cascades and vistas cut through the woodlands, would we even be able to detect the presence of the landscape-gardening element in the description. Thomson, in short, is more intent on seeing the beauty of the expanse in his own way than in emphasizing those of its features which derive from a popular landscape style.[1] This statement is particularly true, also, of *Autumn*, which Miss Manwaring significantly dismisses with the remark that its 'landscapes are well constructed, but less Italian.' In this part of the poem, indeed, Thomson's faculty for massing skilfully observed effects of colour, movement and sound into complex yet harmonious designs is seen at its best. Sir Edmund Gosse has aptly compared his description of the 'imbrowned' autumn woods to Wilson's sombre manner of painting; and Wilson, it will be recalled, was an artist who after six years of assiduous study and painting of landscapes in Italy, returned to find the inspiration for his individual style among the mountains of North Wales. Similarly Thomson's unforgettable rendering of the phantasmal effects of the 'blunted' sun 'glaring' through autumnal mists, though in conformity with the plan of the work it is endowed with as much 'general' truth as is manageable,[2] has a marked and felicitous suggestion of his own borderland scenery about it.

On the whole, then, we may conclude that in Thomson's poetry the passages which are reminiscent of Claude and Salvator are few in comparison with those in which his impressions of nature are individual and his renderings original. Most of his pictorially-influenced descriptions have, besides, distinctive touches that redeem them from artificiality, in which respect he is notably different from some of his imitators.

If the Popian style lends itself to Claude-like descriptions, while Thomson's comprehensive eye delights in the variety of natural beauty more than in the appeal of any one type of landscape, the poetry of the Gray-Warton-Collins group tends rather towards the Salvatorial manner in its treatment of nature. The writers of this school were enthusiasts for the Gothic and the picturesque, and as they favoured the

[1]Christopher Hussey, in his *The Picturesque* (p. 42) quotes from a letter of Thomson describing the park. He is most charmed with 'its sweet embowered retirements, and particularly with a winding dale that runs through the middle of it.' But he makes no reference to the pictorial or landscape-gardening elements of the scene.

[2]E.g. the sun 'frights *the nations*.'

irregularity of the ode in preference to the smooth couplet, so they chose to envisage scenes similar to, if not inspired by, the rugged landscapes of Salvator. Thus Gray, for instance, found Kent's gardening designs too classical, and preferred a landscape that would harmonize with Gothic ruins, while Joseph Warton, whose admiration for Salvator has already been mentioned, exclaims in his *Enthusiast*:

> can Stow,
> With all her Attic fanes, such raptures raise,
> As the thrush-haunted copse, where lightly leaps
> The fearful fawn the rustling leaves along,

and chooses in preference to Versailles such a typically Salvatorial scene as:

> . . . some pine-topt precipice
> Abrupt and shaggy, whence a foamy stream,
> Like Anio, tumbling roars;

Yet it is hardly surprising that neither Gray nor Collins figure largely in Miss Manwaring's study. For they were both lyrical poets of 'extreme conciseness of expression,' and their effects are gained by suggestion rather than by outright description. Touches which recall Salvator occur among Gray's poems, but the lines which seem to bear the closest resemblance to this painter:

> On a rock, whose haughty brow
> Frowns o'er old Conway's foaming flood,
> Robed in the sable garb of woe,
> With haggard eyes the Poet stood;
> (Loose his beard, and hoary hair
> Stream'd, like a meteor, to the troubled air)[1]

were suggested in fact by a picture of Raphael's, as Gray's note testifies.

Collins is generally regarded as one of the very few poets in the eighteenth century who had any genuine understanding of nature. In the *Ode to Evening* the objects described and the personal emotion of the poet are indistinguishably fused, and because of this intensity of expression his poetry is too often regarded as a standard by which the non-lyrical nature poetry of the period is found wanting. For this reason, and also because his verse stands in no need of a revaluation, we may confine our treatment of

[1] *The Bard.*

Collins in this inquiry to the few following remarks on the question of his affinities with landscape art. It will be recognized that there is little 'landscape' in the ordinary sense in the *Ode to Evening*, hardly any scenery in the Highlands Ode, and nothing pictorial in 'How sleep the Brave.' Yet in all of them the feeling of a fresh and delicate response to the beauty of nature is unmistakable.

Two passages in his poetry however come fairly close to Salvator, though whether any reminiscence, conscious or unconscious, of the painter is present in them is purely a matter for conjecture. The first occurs in the *Ode on the Poetical Character*:

> High on some cliff, to Heav'n up-pil'd,
> Of rude Access, of Prospect wild,
> Where, tangled round the jealous Steep,
> Strange Shades o'erbrow the Valleys deep,
> And holy *Genii* guard the Rock,
> Its gloomes embrown, its Springs unlock,
> While on its rich ambitious Head,
> An *Eden*, like his own, lies spread.

The other is to be seen in the first version of the *Ode to Evening*:

> Then let me rove some wild and heathy Scene,
> Or find some Ruin 'midst its dreary Dells,
> > Whose Walls more awful nod
> > By thy religious Gleams.

It has been well said that the changes in the *Ode to Evening* reflect the transition from an outworn poetic style to the more vital expression of a new age; it may also be observed that in the perfected poem Collins casts aside conventional Salvator-resembling images and replaces them by a wonderful evocation of English upland country made strange in the uncertain gleams of an evening sky. One of the happy properties of the poem is its combination of general twilight transfigurations with touches of fidelity to local aspects of nature, and if, as Mr. Blunden thinks, the 'upland fallows grey' of the rewritten stanza help us to assign the scene to the Winchester-Chichester district, this affords us another instance in eighteenth-century nature poetry of local observation tending to remove all traces of pictorial imitation. There was, however, no need for

Collins to de-Salvatorize the appearance of the first-quoted passage, since in this ode he was not aiming at a direct representation of nature but required an illustrative background to enhance the association of ideas, and the forbidding steepness of the ascent to the Miltonic Paradise is sufficiently well conveyed for the purpose in view.

Yet if Collins's affinities with a type of landscape art are to be considered, they may best be estimated not by the surface similarities which isolated quotations provide, but by his predilection for certain tones and moods of nature, by the kind of scenes which his poetry suggests to the inward eye. Here there is fairly ample room for diversity of impression; thus Swinburne proclaims his general likeness to Corot, whose delicate softness Collins certainly shares, though there is also discernible in him a quality of intimacy that the painter lacks. Mr. Laurence Binyon suggests that the *Ode to Evening* might be a counterpart to a drawing by J. R. Cozens, though we may except to this that while Collins has some of Cozens's liking for wild and secluded places, he dwells on the small and revealing circumstances of a scene instead of aiming at a grandeur of total effect. Mr. Blunden, who has written of Collins with more sensitive insight than most critics, feels that 'he has seen our English evening as Claude saw the Enchanted Castle,' but we may infer that he has in mind the mythological aura in which Collins invests the poem rather than the kind of landscape which may be imaginatively evoked from it. If the present writer may be permitted to offer a parallel, it seems to him that the work of the English water-colourist Girtin affords a particularly suggestive comparison with that of the poet. Girtin like Collins combined topographical depiction with lyrical impressionism; his picture of 'The White House on the Thames' and his views of the Wharfe are faithful to nature, yet have a luminous quality of their own which is enhanced by a rhythmic treatment of spaces of light and air. His realization of the potentialities of water-colour for capturing nuances of tone and obtaining an effect of rapid improvisation may be compared with Collins's resort to lyrical measures in preference to the couplet and blank verse in order to obtain similar instantaneous effects. His pictures have Collins's subdued tones and his pale light. In their liking for remote solitudes and ruins they may be considered as precursors of 'Romanticism,' but the beneficent influence of the age is still to be seen in their absence of over-statement and the truth of atmosphere which they maintain.

Collins shared with the Wartons an enthusiasm for Milton's early poems, and his *Ode to Pity* and *Ode to Fear* end in the manner of *L'Allegro* and *Il Penseroso*:

> And I, O Fear, will dwell with thee.

But apart from these there are few traces in Collins of verbal borrowings, and what he takes from Milton he usually sublimates in the process of a fresh poetic creation. With the Wartons, on the other hand, it must be remembered that we are dealing principally with derivative verse. They are the chief representatives of the '*Il Penseroso* school' and as such it is natural to suppose that the source of their inspiration would be more bookish than pictorial. The cheerful openness with which they commit their depredations on Milton's twin poems is at first disarming; but the variations on the borrowed theme are apt to become tiresome owing to their insufficiency of variety and undue length. Occasionally however one of the family pens a poem in this vein in which the sustaining Miltonic element is almost dispensed with, and we have as a result a piece like the younger Thomas Warton's *The First of April*, where the author's genius for close and sympathetic observation of nature has free play.

In all three Wartons it is noteworthy that descriptions akin to Salvator's landscapes are almost entirely absent from the passages (or, more rarely, complete poems) in which the Miltonic manner is temporarily forgotten. One of the rare exceptions occurs in the younger Thomas Warton's blank verse poem, *The Pleasures of Melancholy*, where though the borrowings from *Comus* and *Il Penseroso* are plentiful, the paragraph that contains the following lines happens to be free from them:

> Unbounded waste! the mould'ring obelisk
> Here, like a blasted oak, ascends the clouds;
> Here Parian domes their vaulted halls disclose
> Horrid with thorn, where lurks th' unpitying thief,
> Whence flits the twilight-loving bat at eve,
> And the deaf adder wreathes her spotted train,—

The lurking bandit and the shape resembling a stricken tree are typical features of a Salvator painting, and it is by no means impossible that the author drew on his pictorial rather than his literary memory for the atmosphere of the description. Generally, however, the deliberately induced *Il Penseroso* mood is sufficient to account for passages which show some resemblance to the landscapes . of the Italian painter; or, if the Miltonic influence is not the only one, the gloomy scenes of the poet Young may have contributed as much as those of Salvator to the effects of the kind.

To quote a few examples in which some resemblance to the painter may be traced; the concluding stanza of the elder Thomas Warton's *Ode Written in a Grotto . . . call'd Ludlow's Cave* contains the following lines:

> Let me therefore ever dwell
> In this twilight, solemn cell;
> For musing Melancholy made,
> Whose entrance venerable oaks o'er shade,
> And whose roof that lowly bends
> With awful gloom my serious thoughts befriends.

A similar picture of troglodyte brooding is to be seen in Joseph Warton's *Ode to Fancy*, a poem in which verbal borrowings from *L'Allegro* and *Il Penseroso* mingle with happily-chosen images of his own:

> Say, in what deep and pathless vale,
> Or on what hoary mountain's side,
> 'Mid fall of waters, you reside,
> 'Mid broken rocks, a rugged scene,
> With green and grassy dales between,
> 'Mid forests dark of aged oak,
> Ne'er echoing with the woodman's stroke.—

The third member of the group, may perhaps be best represented in the present connection by another passage from *The Pleasures of Melancholy*:

> Beneath yon ruin'd abbey's moss-grown piles
> Oft let me sit, at twilight hour of eve,
> Where through some western window the pale moon
> Pours her long-levell'd rule of streaming light;
> While sullen sacred silence reigns around,
> Save the lone screech-owl's note, who builds his bow'r

Amid the mould'ring caverns dark and damp,
Or the calm breeze, that rustles in the leaves
Of flaunting ivy, that with mantle green
Invests some wasted tow'r.

But here, as in most of the younger Warton's verse, it is probable that the Salvator-resembling paraphernalia of ruins and caves are sufficiently explicable in terms of his combined enthusiasm for Milton's early poems (shown above by the infiltration from *Comus* in the fourth line) and for everything pertaining to the Gothic.

The writers so far discussed have been selected on account of their merits and fame; and our object has been to show firstly that the better nature-poets were less influenced by landscape painting than has been alleged, and secondly that where imitation appears in their work it is seldom mechanical or due to a poverty of individual perception. An abundance of lifeless pastiche is to be found among the minor versifiers however, particularly during the latter part of the century when the cult of the picturesque had been stimulated by travel-writers such as Brown, Gilpin, and Hutchinson. Many of these, as Miss Manwaring notes, resort to the practice of describing their landscapes with the help of the artists' names; Richard Cumberland, Scott of Amwell and Samuel Rogers in particular show a partiality for alluding to Claude, Poussin and Salvator in order to emphasize their effects. It was in their time, also, that the Claude-glass became popular among the connoisseurs of scenery.

This device, in the form of a convex pocket mirror, or of a curved transparent glass tinted with two or three colours, artificially converged the objects of view on to its surface and tinged them with soft hues. It accompanied many travellers on their visits to the newly or recently-discovered scenery of the Lake District, the Highlands and the Welsh mountains. We may consider that its use denoted a defect of sensibility on the part of the eighteenth-century devotees of the picturesque, and an inability to perceive Nature's way of composing her own scenes. But while this may be admitted it should also be allowed that the less gifted observers were likely to benefit from a contrivance which at least afforded them a concentration of interest. In illustration of its harmless artificiality the Claude-glass might be compared with the modern practice of flood-lighting. In both we have distortion, but the interest aroused in the objects is a genuine one. Architectural masterpieces were no more designed to reveal themselves in a searchlight glare from selected angles than the steeps of the Lake Fells were created to be dwarfed in the reflection of a gentleman's pocket mirror. But in neither instance is the distortion more than playfully experimental.

While the dilettantes probably gained something from their use of the Claude-glass, it is unlikely that the more sensitive observers allowed it to obscure their individuality of vision. We should never know from his poetry that Gray carried a Claude-glass about with him on his travels; though we might easily infer that Erasmus Darwin used one to help him put together his scenic constructions. The latter were produced in conformity with his somewhat eccentric notion that descriptive poetry was a process of painting to the eye, and should secure its effects by a combination of exclusively visual images. His theory is stated and exemplified in *The Botanic Garden* 1789-91, from which we may quote one of his 'got-up' landscapes that is strongly reminiscent of Claude:

> High rocks opposing o'er the stream project
> Their naked bosoms, and the beams reflect;
> Wave high in air their fringed crests of wood,
> And checker'd shadows dance upon the flood;
> Green sloping lawns construct the sidelong scene,
> And guide the sparkling rill that winds between . . .
> Dim hills behind in pomp aerial rise,
> Lift their blue tops, and melt into the skies.

The *fin-de-siècle* descriptive versifiers also include a class of writers who, while they avoid direct imitation of any painter, show their dependence on landscape art by the laboured artifice with which they group together and depict at unnecessary length the several features of their scenes. John Scott is one of these, and a passage from his *Amwell* may be taken as fairly representative of the type:

> How picturesque the view! where up the side
> Of that steep bank, the roofs of russet thatch
> Rise mix'd with trees, above whose swelling tops

Ascends the tall church tow'r, and loftier still
The hill's extended ridge: how picturesque!
Where slow beneath the bank the silver stream
Glides by the flowery isle. . . .

Here the exclamations seem to betray the author's misgiving
as to whether the immediate effect on the eye of a harmonious whole can be convincingly rendered in verse by means
of a succession of descriptive statements.

The practice of looking at nature under the aspect of a
preconceived design is illustrated in the travel-books of the
Rev. William Gilpin, to whom we have already referred.
River-scenes, which he preferred, were divisible into 'four
grand parts: the area, which is the river itself; the two side-
screens, which are the opposite banks, and lead the perspective; and the front screen, which points out the windings of
the river.' Ruthless elimination of particulars, and even of
prominent objects when they interfered with a balanced
composition, is accountable for the empty generalization of
his sepia-tinted drawings; these however have secured him
a place, if an inconspicuous one, among the classical (as
distinguished from the 'topographical') school of water-
colourists.

Examples of this kind in both prose and verse might be
multiplied almost indefinitely, and here the study of
pictorial influences may be given free rein, but the value of
the discoverable resemblances would seem to be confined to
providing a playground for the literary antiquarian. It is
hoped however that sufficiently varied illustrations have been
given to make clear the necessity for distinguishing those
poets who have a love of nature for its own sake from those
who regard it as an elegant background to be filled in after
an approved landscape or bookish manner. Among the
better poets we may indeed discern occasionally a sense of
pleasurable recognition that the configurations or atmosphere
of a certain scene recall beauties made familiar to them by
painting, but there is no straining to look for these effects
everywhere, and no desire to distort (or 'select and improve')
nature until it resembles a distinct style of landscape art,
whether foreign or English.

With these conclusions in mind, let us return for a while
to the *Laokoon* in order to decide how far Lessing's general

objections against descriptive poetry may be considered valid.

IMPLICATIONS OF LESSING'S LAOKOON

However much we may disagree with the full implications of its doctrine, the importance of this work as a landmark in theoretical criticism can hardly be over-estimated. It is, or should be, valued less on account of the attainment of its avowed object—the definition of the essential differences between poetry and painting and the establishment of the autonomy of the former art—than for the original manner in which its author approaches the subject (even though he borrows plentifully from previous writers on the *ut pictura poesis* doctrine, such as Caylus and Shaftesbury) and for the illuminating principles which he evolves in the course of his discussion. To give a pertinent example of the latter, we may quote the following:

> The poet does not merely wish to be intelligible; the prose writer is contented with simply rendering his descriptions clear and distinct, but not the poet. He must awaken in us conceptions so lively, that, from the rapidity with which they arise, the same impression should be made upon our senses which the sight of the material objects that these conceptions represent would produce. In this moment of illusion we should cease to be conscious of the instruments—his words—by which this effect is obtained.

Here he produces a criterion by which the poet, in most forms of verse, may be known from 'the man of rhymes'; it has since become a commonplace of criticism, but the capacity to put forward the idea in his own time, when

A thousand handicraftsmen wore the mask
Of Poesy

gives an indication of the keenness of his critical insight. In modern writing we not infrequently meet with the view that he excels in analytical reasoning, but pays too much attention to the objective and too little to the subjective characteristics of the two arts. Irving Babbitt, for instance, in *The New Laokoon* (pp. 116–7) in order to draw as striking a

contrast as possible between the neo-classic and the romantic
conceptions of 'illusion,' finds it convenient to agree with
the allegation of Lessing's contemporary critic Herder that
Lessing overlooks the suggestive quality of words in poetry;
and maintains elsewhere that 'what we find in the *Laokoon*
is not primarily an appeal to taste and feeling, but a mixture
of Aristotelean theory and precise linguistic and antiquarian
research.' But the quotation we have just given from the
Laokoon should in itself be enough to mitigate this impression, and Lessing has many other remarks in the same vein:
such as his insistence on the fact that a poetical picture is
one which presents itself to the 'inner eye,' and is not likely
to be transferable on to canvas; and his exclamation 'Paint
for us, ye poets, the delight, the affection, the love, the
rapture which beauty produces, and you have painted beauty
itself,' with his accompanying apt illustration of this kind of
description in Ovid's picture of Lesbia. Indeed from the
standpoint of general æsthetics it might be held that he is,
if anything, too solicitous for concentration and intensity of
descriptive expression in poetry. Thus he considers that
since 'succession of time is the department of the poet, as
space is that of the painter,' prolonged descriptions are only
admissible if they introduce the element of action, and
thus become 'progressive pictures,' such as Homer's
account of the making of Achilles' shield.[1] But for a stationary description to be successful, 'the several features, representing the various parts and properties in space,' must
'follow one another with such speed and condensed brevity
that we fancy that we hear all at once.' The effect of these
propositions, strictly applied, would be to rule out of the
sphere of legitimate art not only much 'nature-poetry'
belonging to the debatable field of eighteenth-century
verse, but also sustained descriptions of acknowledged
merit from the poetry of the previous age. Many passages
in Milton (whose poetry Lessing greatly admired) would

---

[1] These principles were kept in view by James Grahame, 'The Cowper of Scotland'
who in the preface to his freshly-observant blank verse poem *The Birds of Scotland*
(1806) remarks: 'In *The Biblical Pictures* I have endeavoured to describe some of
those scenes which painters have so successfully presented to the eye. I need hardly
say, however, that, by the adoption of this title, I meant not to subject myself to
the principles of the art of painting. I have not confined myself to the objects of
sight, nor adhered to one point of time. I have often represented a series of incidents;
and, in portraying characters, I have made them speak as well as act.'

fail to satisfy his theoretical requirements. The famous description of Eden in the fourth book of *Paradise Lost*, copiously suggestive of the pristine beauty of an extensive natural seclusion in its profusion of sights, sounds, tastes and odours, is devoid of both 'action' and 'speed and condensed brevity' of imagery. Perhaps Lessing might have partly justified it from that portion of his theory which asserts the validity of 'musical pictures' in poetry—one which is capable of a wider development than he has given it, especially as applied to the poetry of his own age.

The frequency with which the nature enthusiasts of the eighteenth century bestow admiration on the Eden passage, together with the numerous verbal borrowings that are made from it in poetry show that it was to some extent regarded as a model for descriptive writing of this kind. It cannot be called a 'composition,' in the sense of a precise poetic suggestion of a visible whole—the idealization appropriate to a description of Eden would be impaired if this were so—but it is noteworthy that its truth of atmosphere is enhanced by generalized imagery and Latinisms of the kind that were adopted in the Popian and Thomsonian descriptive poem respectively. Thus on the one hand we have a plentiful use of seemingly vague plurals—Trees, Lawns, Downs, Grots, Caves—together with conventional phrases such as 'purple Grape,' 'tender herb,' and 'murmuring waters,' and on the other, sonorous Latinisms like 'irriguous,' 'imbround', and 'umbrageous' that often reappear in *Cider*, *The Seasons*, and their successors. A good example of an eighteenth-century tribute to the animating power of the passage occurs in Horace Walpole's *Essay on Gardening* (1771)—'The description of Eden is a warmer and more just picture of the present style [of gardening] than Claud Lorrain could have painted from Hagley or Stourhead.'[1] From this the reflection naturally arises that the poets who plundered Milton for their descriptive language may have obtained

[1]In associating the natural wildness of the Eden setting with the freer style of gardening which came in during the early part of the eighteenth century, Walpole had been preceded by Stephen Switzer (in *Ichnographia Rustica*, 1718) and by William Mason (in *The English Garden*, 1767–72). They all doubtless fastened eagerly on to the lines in which Milton appears to disparage the formal garden, viz.:
Flours worthy of Paradise which not nice Art
In Beds and curious Knots, but Nature boon
Powrd forth profuse on Hill and Dale and Plaine.

their landscape suggestions more from him than from the Italian painters.

To return to our subject, if the rigour of Lessing's poetic standards is partly excusable on the score of his zeal for the advancement of a new theory, it should also be held in his favour that the state of contemporary German poetry was such that he felt a drastic corrective to false taste to be necessary. In reaction from the artificiality of the preceding Second Silesian school, a group of 'picturesque' poets had risen to prominence during the first half of the eighteenth century. Its chief members were Brockes, the uninspired translator of Thomson, Kleist, the author of *Frühling* (which draws heavily on Brockes's translation), and Haller whose *Die Alpen* (1732), while independent of Thomson, was specially assailed by Lessing on account of its representative shortcomings. These poets have in common a partiality for exhaustive descriptions of outdoor scenes and occupations, a fondness for prosaic didacticism, and a tendency to lose sight of the whole in their attention to dispersive detail. While it was desirable, as Lessing argued, that a poetry whose motif was action should replace these forms and re-invigorate the national literature, the theoretical value of the *Laokoon* is thereby lessened, owing to its author's special preoccupations. His theory did much more good than harm, but it is too exclusive. An insistence on the element of movement as the one quality that may justify the existence of the long descriptive or descriptive-didactic poem would deprive of poetic rank writers we could do without, such as Erasmus Darwin, but also those we could ill afford to spare, such as Cowper. In an early chapter of the *Laokoon*, Lessing states that 'Nothing is more deceitful than laying down general laws for our feelings. Their web is so fine and complicated, that it is scarcely possible even for the most cautious speculation to take up clearly a single thread and follow it amidst all those which cross it.' *De te fabula*, we feel inclined to add, even though we may allow that for the most part his critical approach is admirably undogmatic.

A question of special interest arises in connection with Lessing's attitude to Thomson. *The Seasons* had a considerable influence in Germany, and it would be natural to expect that its author would figure largely in the *Laokoon*. Yet the references to him there are meagre. This is the more surprising when we take into account that Lessing in his youth had been captivated with Thomson's poetry, and that he bestowed high praise on it in his sketch of Thomson's life.[1] The significance of the scarcity of references to him in the *Laokoon* is ambiguous, and there are two schools of thought on the subject, neither of whose explanations are completely satisfactory. It is maintained on the one hand that by his strenuous campaign on behalf of action and movement Lessing was really preparing the way for a period of renewed activity in the drama, and that the *Laokoon* represents a revulsion from his youthful enthusiasm for the nature-poetry of Thomson, and so from all descriptive poems of lesser merit. There is an element of truth in this; it is certain that he was devoting much of his time to the drama—*Minna von Barnhelm* and the *Laokoon* date from the same period— and it is probable that the newer interest tended to thrust the other into the background. But how far he had come to look askance at *The Seasons* is quite conjectural; the scarcity of allusions to Thomson proves nothing, while those there are, it should be noted, are not of an unfavourable character. On the other hand it is contended that Lessing was occupied in exposing the weaknesses of descriptive poetry, not in discussing its better qualities, and that criticism of Thomson would have been foreign to his purpose. According to this view, the arguments by which he would have justified Thomson are easily discerned. 'L'objet même du poème des "Saisons"', says M. Léon Morel, the author of the fullest study of Thomson that has yet been made, 'c'est cette série de transformations qui entraîne le monde des choses à travers les diverses heures de la journée et différentes saisons de l'année.' In the opening lines of the *Hymn*, which state the theme of the whole poem, the ever-altering appearance of the outward garment of nature is emphasized:

> These, as they change, Almighty Father, these
> Are but the varied God.

It may be further observed that Thomson does not solely convey the impression of change and motion by depicting a succession of stationary pictures; the individual scenes are

[1] In his *Theatralische Bibliothek*.

themselves often composed of evanescent appearances
merging one into another in the act of description. The dawn-
picture in *Summer* (43 sq.) with its shifting lights and colours,
its transference of attention from each typical yet closely
observed object to its successor in time, and its felicitous
glimpses, such as:

> . . . from the bladed field the fearful hare
> Limps, awkward

well illustrates this peculiarity; but the same kind of
artistry may be seen to advantage in other outstanding
passages, such as those portraying the transit of gales and
rainstorms in *Autumn* (330 sq., 993 sq.), and the description
of the thaw in *Winter* (988 sq.). It should be noticed, moreover, that in treating particular localities, where changing
atmospheric effects are less appropriate and stationary
landscapes are liable to ensue, Thomson introduces the
element of movement by conducting his reader up some
slope from which the view may be seen, and then stressing
the quickness with which the eye sweeps over the whole.
Thus, for a view of the country surrounding London we are
invited (in *Spring* 108 sq.) to:

> . . . ascend
> Some eminence, Augusta, in thy plains,
> And see the country, far diffused around,
> One boundless blush, one white-empurpled shower
> Of mingled blossoms; where the raptured eye
> Hurries from joy to joy.

The same method is employed in the Hagley Park
'prospect':

> Meantime you gain the height, from whose fair brow
> The bursting prospect spreads immense around;
> And snatched o'er hill and dale, and wood and lawn,
> . . . your eye, excursive, roams.

These are undeniably artistic merits, and it is probable that
a recognition of them has prompted those who consider
that their author was not included in the scope of the general
charges advanced in the *Laokoon* to claim that Lessing, if he
had seen fit, would have defended Thomson's descriptive
method in the way that he justified the passage in which
Homer described Achilles' shield—'not as finished and

complete, but as it is being wrought . . . thereby converting a tedious painting of a body into a vivid picture of an action.' Yet there is still room for doubt. The kind of extensive description which Lessing allows, has a 'movement' associated with human activity (which cannot be said of most of Thomson's descriptions), while the briefer type, which he prefers, wherein a whole scene is conjured up by the use of the suggestive word or image, is not often met with in Thomson's diffuse and leisurely style. Exceptions are to be found, of course, in both kinds; thus the human element is pronounced in the animated pictures of trout-fishing and sheep-shearing in *Spring* and *Summer*, while an occasional magical phrase like:

> And of gay castles in the clouds that pass
> For ever flushing round a summer-sky

brings to mind Lessing's remarks on the change of beauty into charm; 'Charm is beauty in motion . . . In poetry [as distinguished from painting, motion] remains what it is, a transitory beauty that we would gladly see repeated. It comes and goes.'[1] But on the whole, we may be tolerably sure that Lessing's view of the matter would have coincided with that held by Johnson, who though recognizing in Thomson such ordered movement as was required for the slow unfolding of the pageant of the seasons, reflected on his poem (in the same manner in which he criticized *Windsor Forest*) that 'Of many appearances subsisting all at once, no rule can be given why one should be mentioned before another; yet the memory wants the help of order, and the curiosity is not excited by suspense or expectation.'

Moreover (to clinch the matter) we have direct evidence that Lessing disapproved of one aspect of Thomson's descriptive technique, though unfortunately there are no means of knowing to what extent he would have distinguished his merits from the shortcomings of his imitators, or what poetic rank he would finally have assigned to him. The *Laokoon* as it stands is a fragment. It was to have been followed by a second and a third part, dealing successively with the relation of music to poetry, and the relations of the various kinds of poetry to each other. The second part

---

[1] *Laokoon*, Chap. XXI. The verse quotation is taken from *The Castle of Indolence*, canto i.

would have included an inquiry into the legitimacy of the opera as a form of art; in the third the superiority of the drama over other forms of verse would have been argued, owing to the larger amount of action that it contains. Among the notes prepared by Lessing for the continuation is one which reads:

> Still more are inanimate beauties forbidden to the Poet. Condemnation of Thomson's pictures.

This suggests that the more tranquil, at least, among Thomson's sustained descriptions would have been ruled out of the sphere of genuine poetry. Yet these figure as frequently as any other type of description in *The Seasons*, and Thomson often obtains his happiest effects by means of them. A well-known passage will afford a good illustration of the type:

> But see the fading many-coloured woods,
> Shade deepening over shade, the country round
> Imbrown; a crowded umbrage, dusk and dun,
> Of every hue, from wan declining green
> To sooty dark.

If such a masterly evocation of the sombre tones and massive shades of Autumn is condemned, so should the theory be that condemns it. We cannot say that 'pure description takes the place' of movement in these lines; the picture does not change before our eyes, but it presages change, in the same way as the tarnishing of the brighter hues is implied in retrospect. Thomson's movement, in short, is not generally of the kind postulated by Lessing, and we may surmise that examples of this sort would have come under the heading of 'inanimate beauties.'

The result of our inquiry into Lessing's attitude to Thomson has been to reinforce what we have already observed concerning the over-exclusiveness of the main theory advanced in the *Laokoon*. That the theory has been carried too far can be more confidently asserted when the author's applications of it are shown to be unacceptable. While we may allow Lessing's criticism the considerable merit of directing our attention to the various methods of poetic description and of inviting us to compare them in their appropriateness for particular purposes, we may still hold that 'movement' though a useful criterion is not an essential one, and that bad descriptions of progressive pictures are as likely to be met with as good ones of stationary scenes.

Glancing back over the whole subject of pictorial description, it may be said that over-concern with surface resemblances in the domain of 'influences' (which may be attributed to Miss Manwaring) and excessive zeal for the advancement of a new theory, however desirable and salutary (which may be imputed to Lessing), both tend to the same result; namely the herding together of good and mediocre poets into one category, whether for praise or blame. It has been our object to remove some of the derogatory implications of these inquiries; to show that there are insufficient grounds for considering that the poets who successfully reproduce the beauties of the visible world within their ken have on the one hand deliberately imitated the effects, or on the other mistakenly adopted the technique, of landscape painters.

CHAPTER V

PRINCIPLES OF VISUAL COMPOSITION IN EIGHTEENTH CENTURY POETRY

BUT having cleared them of indebtedness, it remains to inquire more closely into the nature of their originality. We are here concerned with the work of the more gifted eighteenth-century nature poets who describe in detail, as distinguished from those who, in the manner of Pope, effectively leave detail to the imagination— loosely speaking, the poets of eye rather than the poets of ear. Can we not disengage from their poetry some commonly shared technical merit, in addition to the element of movement, which establishes it in its own right and separates it on the one hand from painting, and on the other justifies it in comparison with the (later) nature-poetry which is the mirror of a mood or of a philosophy?

In presenting a picture in terms of language a poet has two advantages over the landscape painter to compensate for the loss of directness which his medium involves. He has in the first place a greater freedom of selection; he need only portray those objects which are necessary to his sense of design, and can ignore or leave to the imagination the intervening stretches of landscape which the painter— generalize he never so wisely—is obliged in some manner to account for. Hence the rapidity of effect, which Lessing rightly stresses, plays its part even in the stationary 'set piece' descriptions which he condemns. Secondly the poet can emphasize the relationships of the various parts of his design in a way denied to the painter, by his complete control over the order in which the objects are presented to us. A large part of the effect of painting depends on the balancing and rhythmic spacing of widely separated colours, masses, and outlines, and as these relationships are not readily perceived, the eye is apt to pause on irrelevant details and so miss the significance of the whole. But the descriptive poet does not incur this risk of misapprehension, for he can conduct our eye over the configurations of his scene in as regular or irregular a course as he pleases. By

combining skilful selection with judicious arrangement
the descriptive poet secures the element of vividness without
impairing the impression of a harmonious whole. The
latter, of course, is a fundamental requirement in both arts,
and it is instructive to note, in this respect, how Sir Joshua
Reynolds and Lessing agree in deriding from their respective points of view the kind of approach to art which might
be styled the botanist's attitude.[1] Yet the botanist's attitude,
in the derogatory sense, is not necessarily applicable even
to pictures and descriptions of 'still life.' Freshness of perception or a feeling for structural relations may unify the
most minutely observed particulars. We see this to advantage
in Crome's small pictures of plants and wild flowers, such
as 'The Burdock,' and realize that there is only a surface
inconsistency between this part of his practice and his
general theory that 'Trifles in nature must be overlooked,
that we may have our feelings raised by seeing the picture
as a whole, not knowing how or why we are so charmed.'
We see it also in those lyrics in which Clare with a joyful
and intimate sense of flower-existence can quicken his field
naturalism into poetry; as for example in *The Primrose
Bank*,

> With its little brimming eye
> And its yellow rims so pale
> And its crimp and curdled leaf,
> Who can pass its beauties by?[2]

For the opposite extreme, for the amorphous verse of the
exactly observing botanist, no better examples could be
found than in Erasmus Darwin's *The Botanic Garden*, that
versified notebook of curious information. A single quotation will suffice:

> While from her bud the playful tulip breaks,
> And young carnations peep with blushing cheeks;

[1]Compare Lessing's condemnation of Von Haller's description of the gentian
(*Laokoon*, XVII) with Reynolds on the misinterpretation of the background of
Titian's *San Pietro Martire* (*Eleventh Discourse*).

[2]Cf. also many felicitous touches in John Langhorne's *Fables of Flora* (1771).
The pansy, for example:

> The tints that stream'd with glossy gold,
> The velvet shade, the purple hue,

or the tulip:

> . . . crimson fading into gold
> In streaks of fairest symmetry.

Bid the closed *corol* from nocturnal cold
Curtain'd with silk the virgin *stigma* fold,
Shake into viewless air the morning dews,
And wave in light its iridiscent hues.
So shall from high the bursting *anther* trust
To the mild breezes the prolific dust:[1]

Keats, who found that in much of Clare's poetry the prevailing idea was apt to be overlaid and stifled by the
description, observed in one of his letters that 'the poet
should have distinctness for his luxury.' This, we feel, is a
counsel of perfection, and it is to be seen operating in the
best nature-poets of the eighteenth century, notably in
Thomson, whose particular images, such as:

And from the bladed field the fearful hare
Limps awkward

often seem to be introduced half-reluctantly, as if their
appeal was too strong to be resisted, not as if they came from
the collection of a methodical naturalist determined to record
everything he has seen. The last-given quotation is indeed
an example of 'that trembling, delicate, and snail-horn
perception of beauty' which according to Keats differentiates
poetic from prosaic observation.

If what has been suggested concerning the special
resources of the descriptive poet is valid, it should follow
that a good poet (of the type we are considering) will be
known from a bad one by his skill in selecting the objects
that best convey the atmosphere of the scene, and by the
design-promoting order with which he marshals them before
us. In order to illustrate this part of the technique of landscape description, let us cull representative passages from
two eighteenth-century poets each of whom has a distinctive
style of his own. First, the placid opulence of the Ouse
valley, as given by Cowper in the well-known lines:

. . . With what pleasure have we just discerned
The distant plough slow-moving, and beside
His labouring team, that swerved not from the track,
The sturdy swain diminished to a boy!
Here Ouse, slow winding through a level plain
Of spacious meads with cattle sprinkled o'er,
Conducts the eye along his sinuous course

[1]*The Botanic Garden*, Part II, canto 4, **xi.**

Delighted. There, fast-rooted in his bank
Stand, never overlooked, our favourite elms
That screen the herdsman's solitary hut;
While far beyond and overthwart the stream
That as with molten glass inlays the vale,
The sloping land recedes into the clouds;
Displaying on its varied side the grace
Of hedge-row beauties numberless, square tower,
Tall spire, from which the sound of cheerful bells
Just undulates upon the listening ear;
Groves, heaths, and smoking villages remote.[1]

With one exception every part of this description has to do with visual appearances, and even the undulating sound of the distant bells suggests something of the kind of country traversed by these notes on their way to the observer—yet we do not feel that the poet has striven to adopt the technique of painting or that his (relatively) slow enumeration has resulted in diffuseness. We receive a harmonious impression of the sort that a good painting of the subject would produce; brought about by means comparable with, though distinct from, those employed by the painter. The pictorial space to be framed depends, with the painter, on the balancing of forms and colours that the scene affords; the poet's boundaries are determined by the assumed capacity of the reader's synthesizing memory. Here, where the subject is an agreeably diversified but prevailingly pastoral view the poet can afford to give a somewhat prolonged and leisurely description and can extend the number of his 'objects' without fear of the confusion that might result were the view made up of bolder and more dramatic contrasts. Yet we do not have to look very closely to perceive that skilful selection has also contributed to the atmosphere of the piece. Thus if we divide the picture into foreground, middle distance, and background, it will be seen that while the distant plane is composed of two portions —one characterized by a single fully described object (the plough) and the other by a cluster of briefly mentioned objects—the two nearer planes are represented by a single feature apiece, the plain of spacious meads, and the group of elms screening the hut. The surroundings of these objects

[1]The view is that which is obtained from the hill-top where the 'Peasant's Nest' used to stand; in the vicinity of Yardley lodge and the park of the Throckmortons.

are largely left to the imagination, but the individual descriptions in themselves readily suggest the probable way in which one stretch of country merges into the next. These interconnections are furthered by the delineation of the course of the river, which in its control over the sequence of appearances also provides the thread whereon much of the design rests. Hence the 'composition' of the landscape is effected by taking the eye in a kind of semicircular sweep over the view; we are first shown the distant figure with his team, and the ploughlands stretching towards us, then the central line of the river along which we look until we pause at the next salient object—the group of favourite elms—and finally the rising ground, which leads the eye back to the horizon here diversified with a multiplicity of objects (including Olney spire and Clifton tower) in reduced scale. The 'beauties numberless' of the variegated plain are wrought into a harmonious whole by the track of our vision being thus rhythmically curved; a haphazard enumeration, on the other hand, would have detracted from the total effect. It may also be observed that the progress from the more open stretches to the plentifully diversified portion of the horizon conveys the impression of variegated spaciousness more effectively than would be produced by a movement in the opposite direction. Whereas in a painting like 'Mousehold Heath' our sight is encouraged to lose itself in the boundless distances of the skyline without the aid of objects lessening on the view, in poetry this method is more difficult of attainment, and it will be found that 'prospect' descriptions, in particular, end almost invariably with a cluster of objects itemized rather than sketched. Cowper's lines are too intimate and leisurely in style to belong to the prospect type, but in so far as they take in the remote horizon they employ that part of the technique, if it may be so called, of the prospect poem.

Let us turn to a passage of a markedly different character; the description of the Carter Fell region steeped in mists, as given in Thomson's *Autumn*:

> Now, by the cool declining year condensed,
> Descend the copious exhalations, checked
> As up the middle sky unseen they stole,
> And roll the doubling fogs around the hill.

No more the mountain, horrid, vast, sublime,
Who pours a sweep of rivers from his sides,
And high between contending kingdoms rears
The rocky long division, fills the view
With great variety; but, in a night
Of gathering vapour, from the baffled sense
Sinks dark and dreary. Thence expanding far,
The huge dusk, gradual, swallows up the plain.
Vanish the woods; the dim-seen river seems
Sullen and slow, to roll the misty wave.
Even in the height of noon oppressed, the sun
Sheds, weak and blunt, his wide-refracted ray;
Whence glaring oft, with many a broadened orb,
He frights the nations. Indistinct on earth,
Seen through the turbid air, beyond the life,
Objects appear; and, 'wildered, o'er the waste
The shepherd stalks gigantic.

Compared with Cowper's Ouse landscape, this picture
appears generalized in treatment, yet it is rarely that we
find Thomson depicting a view that is not explicitly topographical in such precise terms as these. It was part of his
plan to avoid the definite grouping of visible objects in the
parts of his poem that are devoted to purely seasonal appearances. His reluctance to present the forms of objects, his
preference for colours, sounds, and atmospheric effects, is
deliberate, and due to his concentration on phenomena of a
universal character. This being so, it may be objected that we
are diverting the poetical intention of the passage when, from
biographical sources, we discover here a memory-picture
of the summit that dominates the Jedwater valley where
his youth was spent, and was 'the mountain' to him rather
than Carter Fell. But the fact that such an identification has
been made in itself shows that the picture is precise enough
to warrant a local attribution. In any case, local suggestions
as felicitous as these who would wish away?—we would as
soon agree to the rejection of the winter robin which took
place in one of the editions, presumably on account of its
obtrusive realism. Commenting on the general indirectness
of Thomson's method, M. Morel ingeniously remarks of
the Carter Fell passage 'Et, chose singulière, cette description (bien sommaire du reste) n'est introduite que pour
constater la disparition de l'objet qu'elle peint.' From which

we may perhaps infer that Thomson veiled the bare contours of his early haunts by way of a seemly compromise. The purely seasonal requirements are satisfied while the semi-topographical impression remains. Just as the personally familiar parts of the Cheviots are universalized, so the steep northern slopes of a jealous border region are in a sense, internationalized by the agency of mist. Those who, like the present writer, have had the opportunity to compare the description with the actual scene, will readily assent that the picture is true to life. How, then, has the precision of suggestion which we claim for it been secured? The lines do not have to be very searchingly considered before we perceive that their effectiveness is largely due to the same kind of artistry that is employed by Cowper in the passage from *The Sofa*. In Thomson the strokes are broader, the grouping of masses is bolder and simpler—in manner similar to a Wilson landscape, while Cowper's style is more akin to that of Crome or Constable—but the underlying principles of selection and arrangement are the same in both poets. A few characteristic yet widely varied features have been chosen in the Carter Fell passage so as to exhibit the essentials of the scene; a mountainous mass separated from rolling sullen moorlands by a wooded river valley. The order in which the objects are described follows the course that would naturally be taken in casting the eye over the view. Arrested first by the dominating height, our vision follows its slope down to the valley and thence up to the wastes which stretch into the distance. In both poets the course followed is rhythmical in line, and in both the impression of depth is secured by leaving the remoter images to the end of the description.

While there may be alternative interpretations of some of the points discussed in these poems, it is of less importance that the analyses which have been attempted should be indisputable in every particular than that they should have helped to establish our main contention. We have tried by means of these examples to place the *ut pictura poesis* maxim on a new footing, so far as concerns eighteenth-century nature poems of detailed description—to show that the 'precise suggestion of a visible whole' which characterizes the best of them is contrived by methods of composition and grouping analogous to, and often identical in aim with those of landscape painting, but purely poetic in substance and execution. An ability to select the essentials of a scene together with a feeling for the structural succession of images enables the descriptive poet in his own way to rival the painter in the achievement of:

> Composition high,
> And just Arrangement, circling round one Point,
> That starts to Sight, binds and commands the Whole.

These principles, if we may now accept them as such, will serve as a guide in helping us to appraise with more understanding the descriptive poetry of other writers of the period. In later chapters we shall attempt a critical valuation of the work of a few poets of the eighteenth century who have been chosen particularly for their discerning use of stock phraseology on the one hand, and for their skill in visual composition on the other.

THE 'PROSPECT' POEM

But before concluding our inquiry into the artistic methods of the poets of eye, something remains to be said of the prospect poem, examples of which have already been referred to. Wider in visual range and more diffuse in style than the commoner type of landscape poem, it has a technique which differs in some respects from that of the former and therefore merits separate consideration. Although the words 'landscape' and 'prospect' were often used interchangeably in the eighteenth century[1] the latter generally carried a connotation of greater extensiveness of view, and we find it appropriated especially by the arts of poetry and landscape gardening. Shenstone in laying out the grounds of the Leasowes 'pointed his prospects' so as to include the steeple of Halesowen Church and other objects which

---

[1] As an example, we may quote the couplet which ushers in the somewhat confused and rambling prospect-description in John Langhorne's *Studley Park*:
> What pleasing scenes the landscape wide displays!
> Th' enchanting prospect bids for ever gaze.

appeared to be distant when seen in relation to his own diminutive but skilfully diversified estate. In something of the same way the reader's glance strikes out at once towards the 'distant spires' that grace the Prospect of Eton College as described in the opening lines of Gray's ode. Shenstone, it will be recalled, differentiated between the 'landscape' that contained as much variety as could be satisfactorily treated in a painting and the 'prospect' whose scope was too great for canvas.[1] It would be reasonable to assume, therefore, that the technique of the genuine prospect poem should be at least as distinct from that of landscape painting as are the artistic methods of the poems we have been discussing.

Grongar Hill is in many ways an ideal example of the prospect poem, and it is significant that this piece, which was censured by the Rev. William Gilpin for its neglect of the principles of pictorial grouping, was composed by Dyer during his early years of landscape painting among the Carmarthenshire hills. The beneficent influence of the sister art—the 'Silent nymph with curious eye'—is manifested in this poem, as in its companion piece, *The Country Walk*, by the author's ability to focus keenly on chosen patches of homely detail, and in his vivid sense of colour. But we may also discern in these poems Dyer's impatience with the limitations of the brush and the pencil. His shunning of formal 'pictorial' composition is deliberate, and due to a realization that there is a type of scene—the disorganized profusion of an infinitely varied countryside viewed from a low mountain-top[2]—that can only be convincingly rendered by a special kind of poetry. The distinguishing characteristic of the prospect poem is its lack of frame. It might be defined as an unframed panorama, and is therefore distinct in species from Cunningham's panoramic *Landscape* with its clearly-

[1]That the word is used in slightly different senses in the foregoing instances does not invalidate the general distinction we have emphasized between the two terms. The prospects of the Leasowes were vantage-points or look-outs directed on to a view; the 'Prospect' of Gray's ode denotes the view received from a distance of Eton College; while the 'prospect' of Shenstone's definition (the commonest use) refers to the visible scene itself.

[2]Gray, in his *Journal in the Lakes*, October 4, 1769, notices the superiority of a view obtained from a low eminence: 'There is an easy ascent to the top, and the view far preferable to that on Castle-hill . . . because this is lower and nearer to the Lake: for I find all points, that are much elevated, spoil the beauty of the valley, and make its parts (which are not large) look poor and diminutive.' William Mason supports this in his note: 'The *Picturesque Point* is always thus low in all prospects.'

marked boundaries. In *Grongar Hill* the absence of frame becomes apparent as the poet climbs the slope and

> The mountains round, unhappy fate!
> Sooner or later, of all height,
> Withdraw their summits from the skies,
> And lessen as the others rise:
> Still the prospect wider spreads,
> Adds a thousand woods and meads,
> Still it widens, widens still,
> And sinks the newly-risen hill.

Perhaps the dazzlement at the endless variety of view from the summit which he conveys in the following lines from *The Country Walk*:

> Oh how fresh, how pure the air!
> Let me breathe a little here;
> Where am I, Nature? I descry
> Thy magazine before me lie!
> Temples!—and towns!—and towers!—and woods!
> And hills!—and vales!—and fields!—and floods!
> Crowding before me, caged around
> With naked wilds, and barren ground

persuaded him that there was something arbitrary in setting precise limits to the extent of the scene to be depicted. The congregation of plural nouns representing things seen at a distance is a marked feature of the prospect poem, while nearby objects are often presented by a cluster of singular nouns.[1] The lack of particularization which this method involves need not, if skilfully managed, result in vagueness, its aim is rather to suggest a hurrying of the eye over the brilliant profusion of the outspread scene. In *Grongar Hill*, however, it is noteworthy that in addition to the enumeration of far and near objects in this manner, there are places where the eye pauses in its circular sweep, in order to observe certain features in detail. This peculiarity

---

[1] In *Grongar Hill* the picking out of separate objects (following on the collective style of description) suggests the depiction of a region nearer to the hill; e.g.,

> The pleasant seat, the ruined tower,
> The naked rock, the shady bower;
> The town and village, dome and farm,
> Each give each a double charm.

The view from the summit of Breaden in *The Fleece* I, 654–9, provides another example of Dyer's use of plurals;

> What various views unnumber'd spread beneath!
> Woods, towers, vales, caves, dells, cliffs and torrent floods.

of the poem impelled the pictorially-judging Gilpin to
complain that the author had treated his scene inconsistently,
that beyond a purple and presumably distant grove he had
presented a castle 'touched with all the strength of a foreground: you see the very ivy creeping upon the walls.' But
there is a marked difference between the purpose of the
occasional particularization of *Grongar Hill* and that of a
poem like *The Seasons*. Many of Thomson's vivid touches
appear to be introduced diffidently, as if it were hoped that
delicacy of observation would atone for their slightly
dispersive effect; Dyer on the other hand relies on these
glimpses to introduce the unifying elements of his poem.
For *Grongar Hill* although frameless is by no means form-
less. The fact that it is unusually long for a prospect description, and the consideration that, unlike most prospect
descriptions it is a separate poem, combine to render it all
the more necessary that there should be some principle of
inner coherence in the piece. This is provided by the meditative strain of wistful reflection on the delusiveness of human
hopes and ambitions, which is ushered in by the detailed
pictures of the ivied ruin and the meads. The latter is
the more effective of the two owing to the felicitous sudden-
ness with which the idea associates itself with the image:

> How close and small the hedges lie!
> What streaks of meadows cross the eye !
> A step methinks may pass the stream,
> So little distant dangers seem;
> So we mistake the future's face,
> Eyed through hope's deluding glass;

These reflections give rise to further description by way of
consolatory contrast:

> Now, even now, my joys run high,
> As on the mountain-turf I lie;

and in this manner the poem while going forward is bound
together into a whole, ending with (what perhaps carries a
suggestion of 'some blessed hope') the woodland-echoing
notes of the thrush.

For the most part, however, prospect descriptions are to
be found as passages embedded in the long poems (usually
of blank verse) devoted to husbandry or laudatory topo-

graphy with which the eighteenth century abounds. As such
they are less dependent on roundedness of form for their
effect, and being concerned with 'pure description' may be
considered to fulfil their aim if they successfully convey the
impression of multitudinous variety taken in at a single
sweep of the eye. A pleasing example of this type of verse
is to be found in the *Edge-Hill* of Richard Jago, the life-long
friend of Shenstone, and author of the better known poem
The Blackbirds. In his prefatory synopsis the poet divides
the territory seen from the hill 'by an imaginary line into a
number of distinct scenes, corresponding with the different
times of the day, each forming an entire picture, and
containing its due proportion of objects and colouring.'
That these sections have the elaborate unity which Jago
claims for them will hardly be allowed, but the contrast
provided by 'The Morning View,' for instance, 'compre-
hending the south-west part of the scene' (which, apart
from the reflective digressions, is depicted with almost the
dutifulness of a cartographer) and the 'General View' which
precedes it, shows with unusual clarity how the style of
applied description differs from that of the 'prospect.' True
to type, Jago's rendering of the latter is introduced by an
'ascent to the summit' of the ridge; whereupon the four
quarters of the horizon are scanned in a wheeling glance:

> The summit's gain'd! and, from its airy height,
> The late-trod plain looks like an inland sea,
> View'd from some promontory's hoary head,
> With distant shores environ'd; not with face
> Glassy and uniform, but when its waves
> Are gently ruffled by the southern gale,
> And the tall masts like waving forests rise.
> Such is the scene! that, from the terrac'd hill,
> Displays its graces; intermixture sweet
> Of lawns and groves, of open and retir'd.
> Vales, farms, towns, villas, castles, distant spires,
> And hills on hills, with ambient clouds enrob'd,
> In long succession court the lab'ring sight,
> Lost in the bright confusion.

It may be said that though the prospect passage (as distinguished from the prospect poem) need do no more than
describe its scene directly, yet its effectiveness is sometimes

enhanced by the inclusion in it of a passing reflection which serves, if not to confer a subjective unity on the view, at least to set the latter in some kind of mental perspective. The presence of this element in what is almost unquestionably the finest prospect in eighteenth-century poetry, the view from Hagley Park in Thomson's *Spring*, should be taken into account in any examination of the peculiar merits of the passage. The lines have often been admired, yet their underlying artistry, though simple, is so unobtrusive as to be likely to escape recognition:

> Meantime you gain the height, from whose fair brow
> The bursting prospect spreads immense around,
> And snatched o'er hill and dale, and wood and lawn,
> And verdant field, and darkening heath between,
> And villages embosomed soft in trees,
> And spiry towns by surging columns marked
> Of household smoke, your eye, excursive, roams;
> Wide-stretching from the hall, in whose kind haunt
> The hospitable genius lingers still,
> To where the broken landscape, by degrees
> Ascending, roughens into rigid hills;
> O'er which the Cambrian mountains, like far clouds
> That skirt the blue horizon, dusky, rise.

The sharp contrast presented by the juxtaposition of the hospitable hall, which lies at the foot of the eminence whereon the observer stands, and the 'broken landscape' of the horizon which 'roughens into rigid hills' brings a tinge of visual adventurousness into what might otherwise be a too placid panorama. It is sometimes objected against eighteenth-century poets that in depicting nature they seldom stray outside the confines of the park or country estate. Though it is rarely that he does so elsewhere, Thomson might seem to incur this objection in the present example. But by introducing into the view the mansion with its associations of security and secluded ease, the poet accentuates the impression of increasing wildness on the distant plane. It is noteworthy, too, that he uses the hall as a kind of radiating point in his description. From the neighbouring Clent hills the view spreads outwards in the direction of the Wrekin in the north and beyond the Malvern hills on the south. With an economical use of apt imagery

Thomson conveys this spreading effect by passing from a nearer group of singular nouns (where each object named stands for an innumerable quantity of these objects)[1] to a clearly marked off group of plural nouns representing the features of the more distant scene. The density of 'objects' to a line, moreover, diminishes evenly as the horizon is approached: thus the crowded profusion of the foreground is conveyed by the swift succession of 'hill and dale, and wood and lawn,' where the rapidity of glance leaves no room for epithets, while in the next line two objects are described with an epithet apiece, and so on, until the attention dwells on a feature here and there that stands out against the indistinctness of the horizon. But just before penetrating to the outermost fringe where the wilder country begins, he reverts to the focal centre and in so doing not only provides the stimulus of contrast but emphasizes the distance travelled by the eye.

The poet confers a further unity on the passage by his skilful management of rhythm and verbal music. The danger of the prospect passage is that it may easily degenerate into a catalogue. But Thomson has avoided such diffuseness by gathering everything into one verse paragraph, as if the whole view were taken in at a single deep breath. The pattern of the verse, accordingly, is that of a comprehensive undulating flow, which is almost arrested at the words 'roams' and 'hills' (marking pauses where the transition from one plane to another takes place) but whose rhythmic momentum enables it to overpass all checks until the full close, or resonant 'climacteric line' is reached. It may also be noted how the element of musical suggestiveness contributes to the total effect; how in the last four lines, for instance, the skilful combination of r-sounds and open and varied vowels conveys the impression of both roughness and remoteness.

The three pieces discussed above have exhibited one characteristic of prospect poetry, the tendency to enumerate rather than describe in detail, which calls for some further comment. The origin of the lists of objects that appear so frequently in eighteenth-century descriptive verse (not only

[1] Hugh Miller, however, in his *First Impressions of England,* estimated the number of fields (which are small and screened by luxuriant hedgerows) at about forty thousand.

in prospect poetry) has been assigned to Milton, and it is by no means improbable that the Thomsonian school of blank verse writers were as impressed as later generations of readers have been by the formidable

> Rocks, Caves, Lakes, Fens, Bogs, Dens, and shades of death

or by lines approximating closer to landscape, such as:

> sweet interchange
> Of Hill and Vallie, Rivers, Woods and Plaines,
> Now Land, now Sea, and Shores with Forrest crownd,
> Rocks, Dens and Caves.

But the better kind of prospect-writers do not employ this device in mere imitation; they adapt it to meet the requirements of their special style of description. Milton's lists encourage the reader to conjure up some purely imaginary scene; they are idealized, non-representational, and even when (as rarely happens) they are used to depict some definite locality, as that of Rome, in *Paradise Regained*:

> With Towers and Temples proudly elevate
> On seven small Hills, with Palaces adorn'd,
> Porches and Theatres, Baths, Aqueducts,
> Statues and Trophees, and Triumphal Arcs,
> Gardens and Groves presented to his eyes
> Above the highth of Mountains interpos'd.[1]

their purpose is more to evoke historical associations of splendour and power than to suggest the configurations of an actual view. Among the Miltonidae it is only poets of intermittent and flagging inspiration, like Young, who attempt to rival their master in composing these shadowily-impressive catalogues; as for example:

> Seas, Rivers, Mountains, Forests, Deserts, Rocks
> The Promontory's Height, the Depth profound,
> Of Subterranean, excavated Grots . . .
> Ev'n these an aggrandizing impulse give;
> Of Solemn Thought enthusiastic Heights
> Even These infuse.

In this school, however, the writers of more sustained originality (as we have seen in Dyer and Thomson, and to a less extent in Jago) put the poetic list to more objective uses. For in addition to perceiving the general appropriate-

[1] iv, 34-9.

ness of the list for the depiction of the chequered profusion of an expanse, these poets nearly always contrive by some slight touch during the process of enumeration—whether by the choice of a distinctive image, such as 'spiry towns,' or by an effective conjunction of objects, such as 'The pleasant seat, the ruined tower'—to communicate something of the *genius loci* of their favoured view. Here, then, we again meet with that essential requirement for the proper interpretation of eighteenth-century nature-poetry, the need to distinguish between the creative and the stereotyped use of a well-established convention.

Many other examples of prospect verse, of varying degrees of merit, might be treated. James Thomson concludes his summer evening effusion on the golden tranquillity of the Thames valley (a landscape and philosophy of contentment in one) with a prospect which though shorter than the Hagley passage has a note of authentic lyrical fervour about it.[1] The prospect in the fifth book of *Sickness*[2] shows William Thompson's indebtedness to the view of the country near London in blossom-time as described by the author of *Spring*, but it is not without some felicitous individual touches. The fecklessly irresponsible Irishman Samuel Boyse (1708–49) who sank to such tragi-comical depths of indigence, and of whom Chalmers relates that frequently 'his friends were surprised to meet the man in the streets to-day, to whom they had yesterday sent relief, as to a person on the verge of dissolution,' wrote several pieces of topographical eulogy in the hopes of securing titled patronage. One of these, entitled *Retirement*, contains a prospect of the wildly-wooded grounds of Yester which, as the present writer can testify, shows a very fair ability in recapturing the scenic effects of the park and its surroundings. In the general prospect which precedes the more detailed description of *Amwell*, John Scott ranges pleasantly over the country near Ware. The passage in question exhibits the familiar marks of this type of verse; the preliminary ascent to the viewpoint and the grouping of singular followed by that of plural nouns, for the depiction of nearby and distant objects respectively.

[1]*Summer*, 1438–41.
[2]Lines 17 sq.

But—to stop short of a compilation of such passages[1]— enough has been said to demonstrate the artistic technique of the prospect description, and to exhibit its purely poetic and individual evolution. It is a sub-species of descriptive verse that has so far escaped literary classification, yet it is not on that account unimportant. For it has been gathered into our poetic tradition, and sometimes reappears in the work of more recent poets, who use it unconscious, perhaps, of its origin, as in such well-known lines as:

> Calm and deep peace on this high wold,
>   And on these dews that drench the furze,
>   And all the silvery gossamers
> That twinkle into green and gold:
>
> Calm and still light on yon great plain
>   That sweeps with all its autumn bowers,
>   And crowded farms and lessening towers
> To mingle with the bounding main.

[1] *The Gentleman's Magazine* (lviii, 151) complained in 1788 that 'readers have been used to see the Muses labouring up . . . many hills since Cooper's and Grongar, and some gentle Bard reclining on almost every mole-hill.'

PART THREE

CHAPTER VI

POPE'S 'PASTORALS' AND 'WINDSOR FOREST'

POPE'S claim to be considered a nature-poet rests on the *Pastorals* and on the non-political part of *Windsor Forest* (the first 290 lines); these were his earliest productions and constitute, it is true, a very small portion of his whole poetic output. Writers who seek to stress the limitations of Pope's genius generally maintain that these poems should be regarded chiefly as brilliant exercises in versification, significant as showing his early concern for symmetry of language and precision of musical effect, but unworthy to rank as genuine nature poems of original merit. Such critics sometimes concede that the *Pastorals* contain faint hints of a passing appreciation of rural beauty—to be seen, for example, in the depiction of the quivering shade cast by the alders—and in view of Wordsworth's commendation a passage or two in *Windsor Forest* —particularly that describing the pheasant—is recognized as showing first-hand observation. For the most part, however, it is alleged that the source of this poetry is to be found in books rather than in direct experience, for line after line of the *Pastorals* is traceable to Virgil's *Eclogues*, while *Windsor Forest* would hardly have been written but for the *Cooper's Hill* of 'majestic Denham.' The *Pastorals* have suffered from under-estimation to a greater extent than *Windsor Forest*. They have been disparaged on the grounds that their passages of dialogue resemble the conversation of coffee-house wits more than the artless exchange of shepherds (regardless of the fact that at the time of their composition, Pope was unfamiliar with coffee-house life); on the other hand they have been decried as 'mere schoolboy exercises'—a more persistent charge, which originates, perhaps, from Warton's unfavourable comparison of Pope's eclogues, in respect of 'invention,' with the compositions of his own pupils at Winchester. Pope may be held to have encouraged this attitude towards his early pieces by the condescending tone with which he speaks of them in the Prologue to the Satires; though it may be remarked that his proclaimed pride in the ousting of 'pure description' by 'sense' probably concealed a feeling of poetic loss, and that he took care in his prefatory notice to reaffirm the flawlessness of their versification.

Of the 'correctness' of the *Pastorals* there has never been any doubt:

> Nor rivers winding through the vales below,
> So sweetly warble, or so smoothly flow.
> Now sleeping flocks on their soft fleeces lie,
> The moon, serene in glory, mounts the sky.[1]

Lines such as these, in which the pervasive but unforced alliteration, the gentle undulation produced by variations of pause, and the languorous but skilfully-modulated vowel-music all contribute to the depiction of the scene, are sufficiently numerous to attest Pope's consummate verse-craftsmanship. The credit of showing Pope the way in which he was likeliest to win renown belongs to Walsh, who pointed out to him that 'though we had several great poets, we never had any one great poet that was correct.' That Pope held to this view, we know from the *Epistle to Augustus*, written many years after Walsh's death:

> Late, very late, correctness grew our care.

Dryden's verse had revealed the capacity of the couplet for precise artistry, though he was too vigorous and impatient a writer to bestow the necessary finish on his lines. Denham, too, though he showed the possibilities of the antithetical structure of the distich, retained some traces of earlier roughness, particularly in his use of rhyme. Waller, who was smoother than Denham, wrote chiefly in the panegyrical vein, and he imparted a false elegance to his style by his over-fondness for mythological decoration. 'Granville the polite' was too admiring an imitator of Waller to make any marked contribution to the process of refinement.

In Walsh, however, Pope could discern a style of writing which, if it were sufficiently cultivated, might yield rich results. Walsh's verse was scanty and occasional, but he had a gift of epigrammatic neatness; he drew largely on the

[1] *Winter*, 3–6.

classics in his *Pastoral Eclogues* and yet avoided slavish imitation, and he rejected the mythological embellishments of Waller and Granville. Moreover Walsh was, in Dryden's estimation, 'the best critic in the nation'; this was of equal importance to Pope, who was able to submit his lines to him for detailed comment. Among the Richardson papers are preserved two manuscripts; one is the copy of the *Pastorals* that passed through the hands of his early patrons, written (conformably with his ideal of impeccable versification) in italics of such neatness as to be scarcely distinguishable from fine printing; the other contains sets of emendations which Pope subsequently offered to Walsh, together with the latter's judgements thereon. On the whole, Walsh chose with remarkable sureness of taste, and some of Pope's happiest strokes owe their establishment to his adviser's discernment. Thus the last two lines of the passage quoted above (which are perfect in their transition from hushed to clearer sounds, in preparation for the shepherd's song) were not shaped until several variants had been rejected by Walsh. Pope also expressed concern lest the constant inlaying of his work with lines translated from the classics should be imputed to him for a lack of originality. In view of the extent to which translation figures amongst his early productions, later critics have been inclined to label all the work of his first period as imitative. Walsh, however, reassured him that the 'best of the modern poets in all languages are those that have the nearest copied the ancients.' At heart, Pope knew that his *Pastorals* were informed with a true creative spirit; as he wrote to Walsh:

> Writers, in the case of borrowing from others, are like trees, which of themselves would produce only one sort of fruit, but by being grafted upon others may yield variety. A mutual commerce makes poetry flourish; but then poets, like merchants, should repay with something of their own what they take from others.[1]

To a large extent the 'something of his own' which Pope bestows on these eclogues is a feeling for his rural environment; for by the effective grouping of groves, winding vales, cooling streams and green retreats so as to satisfy the reader's sense of aural harmony, he contrives to evoke the

[1] July 2, 1706.

serene opulence of a fertile well-wooded English landscape.
In his *Discourse on Pastoral Poetry* he observes that:

> Nothing more conduces to make these composures natural,
> than when some knowledge in rural affairs is discovered. This
> may be made to appear rather done by chance than on design,
> and sometimes is best shown by inference; lest by too much
> study to seem natural, we destroy that easy simplicity from
> whence arises the delight.

The passage may be regarded as a key to the proper appreciation of the *Pastorals*, for it shows how highly Pope valued
concealed or subordinated particularity in this kind of
nature-poetry. As to his familiarity with the spacious glades
and woodlands surrounding his home at Binfield (which has
been questioned by anti-Popians on the score of his physical
disability) we know from his letters that he went for rambles
in the country with his dog, that he delighted in the song of
birds, and that he took solitary reflective walks by moonlight;[1] while from Spence we may infer that the decision to
compose the *Pastorals* was made during the time of his daily
rides in the forest with Sir William Trumbull. Moreover it
can hardly be doubted that the following lines in *Windsor
Forest* (though they are indebted to the reflections of Virgil
and Horace on the philosophy of a country life) have a
reference to his own pursuits and meditations:

> Happy the man . . .
> Whom humble joys of home-felt quiet please,
> Successive study, exercise, and ease.
> He gathers health from herbs the forest yields,
> And of their fragrant physic spoils the fields:
> With chemic art exalts the min'ral pow'rs,
> And draws the aromatic souls of flow'rs:
> Now marks the course of rolling orbs on high;
> O'er figured worlds now travels with his eye;
> Of ancient writ unlocks the learned store,
> Consults the dead, and lives past ages o'er:
> Or wand'ring thoughtful in the silent wood,
> Attends the duties of the wise and good.

In some respects, Pope's Binfield period shows a curious
resemblance to Milton's Horton period. Both were phases
of rural seclusion, of omnivorous reading and of fervid

[1] Cf. Pope's well-known rendering of the moonlight scene in the *Iliad*, VIII, *ad fin.*

mental activity; both poets produced short pieces of keen and brilliant quality, and both were preparing themselves for more sustained flights. But while Milton's wings were strong enough to withstand being ruffled and impaired during his public career, Pope's flight never took place. Instead, by purveying more and more to the taste of the town, he allowed his genius to become canalized. Joseph Warton (though he was too much swayed by Miltonic preoccupations to form a just estimate of *Windsor Forest* and the *Pastorals*) was near the mark when he asserted that 'Whatever poetical enthusiasm Pope actually possessed, he withheld and stifled.'

The enthusiasm for nature is more easily perceived in *Windsor Forest*, where the description is direct, than in the *Pastorals*, where it is incidental. In the latter, we have 'nature to advantage dressed,' and the ruling principle appears to be:

> Let not each beauty everywhere be spied,
> Where half the skill is decently to hide.

Much of the effect of these pieces depends on the unforced pervasiveness of their landscape setting. It is a setting composed chiefly of trees; on all sides there is a generous growth of deciduous foliage, skirting the valleys and climbing the hills of the royal domain. Even in *Spring*, where the scene is an open valley stretching towards a 'furrow'd plain,' the glimpses we receive of osiers and oaks and woodbine bowers show that the woodlands are close at hand.[1] From the summit of the hill in *Autumn* we descry in the sunset glow fields and peacefully smoking villages commingled with groups of limes and knotted oaks; we see yellow groves flecked with red berries, and pick out the poplar on whose rind the shepherd carved his 'amorous vows.' The moonlit grove of *Winter* is touched with frost, and the dropping trees are hung with pearls. In *Summer* we are on the bank of a stream, but our eyes are drawn towards different kinds of shade, the shade of the beeches, the quivering shade of the alders, the shade of the thickets in which the flocks seek

---

[1]Spring is also the season depicted in an earlier-composed pastoral entitled *Palaemon*, which Mr. Norman Ault (*Pope's Own Miscellany*, 1935) has recently enabled us to include among Pope's works. Pope drew from it several phrases and images for use in the other pastorals. It has not their unity of expression, but its setting of groves, shades, and 'dancing osiers' betokens its woodland origin.

respite at noon, the deep forest-shades haunted by 'chaste Diana,' the crowding shade of the over-arching glade which invites the shepherd's absent love. The well-known lines in *Summer* ('Where'er you walk', etc.), which are so faultless in their golden felicity that they were chosen by Handel for the serenely-proportioned strains of the air in *Semele*, provided the occasion for one of the most obtuse of Ruskin's frequent misjudgments. Having bid us hear 'the cold-hearted Pope' say these lines 'to a shepherd girl,' he adds in tones of high-minded reprobation:

> This is not, nor could it for a moment be mistaken for, the language of passion. It is simple falsehood, uttered by hypocrisy; definite absurdity, rooted in affectation, and coldly asserted in the teeth of nature and fact. Passion will indeed go far in deceiving itself; but it must be a strong passion, not the simple wish of a lover to tempt his mistress to sing.[1]

Insensitiveness to the qualities of a little masterpiece of conventionalized style could go no further.

The lines in question did not reach their full perfection until various earlier attempts had been discarded. The original manuscript version reads:

> While you your presence to the grove deny,
> Our flowers are faded, and our brooks are dry;
> Though with'ring herbs lay dying on the plain,
> At your return they shall be green again.

Dissatisfied with this passage, Pope submitted the following variants to Walsh:

> Winds, where you walk, shall gently fan the glade,

Or:

> Where'er you walk, fresh gales shall fan the glade,
> Trees, where you sit, shall crowd into a shade,
> Flow'rs where you tread in painted pride shall rise,

Or:

> Where'er you tread, the purple flow'rs shall rise,
> And all things flourish where you turn your eyes.

The latter well earned the designation of 'knowing' which Pope later bestowed on him, by selecting the versions nearest to those which (with the substitution of 'cool' for 'fresh,' and 'blushing' for 'purple') were finally adopted. As a corrective

[1] *Modern Painters*, Part IV, Chap. XII, 'The Pathetic Fallacy.'

to the view that Pope employed his stock epithets in a perfunctory or mechanical manner, we would do well to notice here how 'cool' is to be preferred to 'fresh,' as having a more assuaging quality (both in sound and sense) and as combining with 'crowd' of the next line to produce a leisurely alliteration, instead of with 'fan' to produce an abrupt one; and how instead of the stiffer 'purple,' the epithet 'blushing' (in assonance with 'flourish' of the next line) contributes to the visual impression of calm luxuriance which it is desired to convey. It cannot be said, then, that in the *Pastorals* Pope's poetic diction becomes a substitute for poetic feeling. Similarly, though the settings are generalized in treatment, the atmosphere of the landscape is vividly present to his mind. Had he wished, he could have much more easily depicted the view from the summit of the hill in *Autumn* in a topographical manner. As it is, we have occasional suggestions of an observed stretch of country—in the commingling of villages, fields and woods, in the configurations of the higher ground, and in the direct allusion 'while Windsor groves admired'—slight in themselves, but sufficient to prevent the pastoral idealization from becoming trivial or monotonous.

For the general design of *Windsor Forest*, Pope was indebted to *Cooper's Hill*, but by adding many felicitous touches of his own, he succeeded in establishing the topographical-didactic poem as a distinct species of eighteenth-century verse. In Denham's poem we find most of the themes or *motifs* which Pope used and rearranged to suit his particular purpose; the invocation, the generalized though not indistinct description, the marshalling of historical and literary celebrities associated with the locality, the condemnation of historical misdeeds enacted there, the description of field sports, the meditation on rural retirement and peace of mind, the praise of thriving agriculture and commerce, and the conclusion on a political note. Some of these *motifs* became especially popular in later verse; the stag-hunt, for example, appears in many of the topographical poems subsequent to *Windsor Forest*, and it is to be found in one of the less numerous local poems—*St. Leonard's Hill*, by R. F. (1666)—that were produced in the period between Denham and Pope. In addition, we find

poet after poet adopting one of Denham's devices for
introducing generalized description; his recognition,
namely, of how Nature composes striking contrasts of scene
into a unity of her own :

> Wisely she [Nature] knew, the harmony of things,
> As well as that of sounds, from discords springs.
> Such was the discord, which did first disperse
> Form, order, beauty through the Universe;
> While driness moysture, coldness heat resists,
> All that we have, and that we are, subsists.
> While the steep horrid roughness of the Wood
> Strives with the gentle calmness of the flood.
> Such huge extreams when Nature doth unite,
> Wonder from thence results, from thence delight.

Thus, to quote a few examples, this reappears in *Windsor
Forest* as :

> Here hills and vales, the woodland and the plain,
> Here earth and water seem to strive again;
> Not chaos-like together crush'd and bruised;
> But, as the world, harmoniously confused:
> Where order in variety we see;
> And where, though all things differ, all agree.

In Francis Fawkes' *Bramham Park* (1745) it becomes :

> At Bramham thus with ravish'd eyes we see
> How order strives with sweet variety:
> Nature, kind goddess, joins the aid of art
> To plan, to form, and finish every part.

And in John Langhorne's *Studley Park* (c. 1750) it is
elaborated as follows :

> Where the fond eye in sweet distraction strays
> Most pleas'd, when most it knows not where to gaze.
> Here groves arrang'd in various order rise
>
> .   .   .   .   .
>
> Here moss-clad walks, there lawns of lively green,
> United, form one nicely-varying scene.

It does not require a very close comparison between
Windsor Forest and *Cooper's Hill* to realize that Pope's most
notable contribution to the topographical *genre* consists of
the richer and more ample vein of nature description which
he introduces into it. In Denham's poem the objects seen

from the hill-top are valued less in themselves than for the
opportunities for discursive meditation that they provide;
in the earlier portion of *Windsor Forest*, however, the pleasurable depiction of rural beauty is more pronounced than the
reflective element. Pope's descriptive style, moreover, is
excellently adapted to the end in view, for though he
retains the generalized word-painting appropriate to a
semi-didactic poem, he skilfully blends it with touches of
individual observation. Thus in illustrating the 'order in
variety' of his landscape, while he dwells on the contrast
between the thicker groves with their chequered light, and
the open lawns and glades dotted with a few trees of slender
growth, he adds a circumstance that is a distinctive feature of
Windsor 'forest'—the proximity (in the neighbourhood of
Bagshot Heath and Chobham Common) of a heathy fir-
wooded country interspersed with cultivated land:

> Ev'n the wild heath displays her purple dyes,
> And midst the desert fruitful fields arise,
> That, crown'd with tufted trees and springing corn,
> Like verdant isles the sable waste adorn.

Joseph Warton, therefore, showed a lack of discernment when
he complained of the poem that 'rural beauty in general,
and not the peculiar beauties of the forest of Windsor, are
here described.'

In historical surveys of eighteenth-century literature we
often find *Windsor Forest* compared disadvantageously with
The Seasons; and Thomson's observant and wide-ranging
eye, his extensive knowledge of natural facts and sensitiveness to unusual effects of colour and atmosphere are brought
forward in order to show how meagre and conventional
Pope appears beside him. But such judgements imply
falseness of perspective; for the two poems belong to different categories, and just as Pope's well-balanced and equable
style of description would be inappropriate to a nature-poem
of the scope of *The Seasons*, so Thomson's copious and
expansive treatment of his subject would, if applied to
Windsor Forest, overcharge the poem and make it unwieldy.
Windsor Forest requires to be viewed in relation to *Cooper's
Hill* in order that its merits may be properly appreciated;
when that is done, we see that Pope is to be praised not only
for his enlargement and enrichment of the descriptive

portion,[1] but also for his artistic control of it, for, to apply to him an apt phrase of Professor Elton's on the workmanship of the best eighteenth-century verse, he shows 'an instinctive refusal to ask too much of the material' coupled with 'a resolve to use the material up to its very limits.' In his treatment of the conventional laudatory reference to poets of recent fame, for instance, we are made aware of a penumbra of real Windsor shades:

> I seem through consecrated walks to rove;
> I hear soft music die along the grove.
> Led by the sound, I roam from shade to shade,
> By godlike poets venerable made:
> Here his first lays majestic Denham sung;
> There the last numbers flow'd from Cowley's tongue.

Pope's faculty for imparting vividness to stock poetic language is abundantly displayed in *Windsor Forest*. In the description of the hunt, for example, we have a couplet in which there is 'not a single new image of external nature':

> See the bold youth strain up the threatening steep,
> Rush through the thickets, down the valleys sweep,

Yet owing to the way in which the stresses are distributed, we can almost feel the horse beneath us gathering his forces for an attempt on the not quite gained summit, and recollect that Pope was regarded by his squire-companions at Binfield as 'no great-hunter, indeed, but a great esteemer of the noble sport, and only unhappy in . . . want of constitution.'[2] Correspondingly, the expression 'the scaly breed' is amply justified in virtue of the carefully-distinguished markings and colours with which Pope variegates the succeeding list of fishes (142–6).

The concluding portion of *Windsor Forest* was written in 1712 at the suggestion of Lord Lansdown, who, as an active Tory, desired a poetical glorification of the Treaty of Utrecht. Six years had elapsed since Pope had completed the first part of the poem, and though he did not finally leave Binfield till 1716, his interests had been increasingly drawn by the literary activities of the London coffee-house coteries. The

---

[1] The extensiveness of the descriptive parts of *Bramham Park* and *Studley Park* (cited above) may be attributed to the influence of *Windsor Forest*. Both of these poems are later in date than *The Seasons*, yet in turns of phrase and choice of nature-imagery they show an exclusive following of Pope's example.

[2] Letter to H. Cromwell, April 10, 1710.

latter part of the poem suggests that he had already lost much of his early enthusiasm for his sylvan surroundings. In its prevailing aspect, it calls to mind the vainglorious rotundities of a contemporary political-allegorical mural painting,[1] and the bevy of personified abstractions at the close readily suggests a ceiling-decoration of sprawling deities. Joseph Warton testifies to the increased artificiality when, in a momentary manifestation of true neo-classic taste, he remarks on the figure of Father Thames that 'the relievo upon his urn is finely imagined.' A brief return to rural scenes is suggested by the agreeably-versified list of tributaries, and since each stream has its descriptive phrase or epithet, it might be supposed that Pope was writing out of a loving familiarity with these haunts. The imagery, however, is almost entirely appropriated from the similar lists of rivers (which include the Thames' tributaries) in Spenser, Drayton and Milton. In this part of the poem Windsor Castle—a symbol of political power and victorious rule— fills up the foreground; and, however much we admire the way in which castle and forest compose in landscape and in actual view, it must be admitted that in Pope's verse they are somewhat uneasy neighbours. Allowance must be made, however, for the fact that here he was, in a sense, writing to order. Hence, though we may be able to discern some atrophying of his feeling for nature, we ought also to recognize the skill with which—following Denham's manner of passing from the stag-hunt near Runnymede to the concluding reflections (coloured by the approaching civil war) on the responsibilities and dangers of kingship—he manages the transition from sylvan strains to the celebration of the triumphs of 'great Anna' and the Tory ministry.

AMBROSE PHILIPS

While Pope was a pioneer in skilful generalized nature description through the medium of the couplet, and John

[1] Cf. 307–10:
Then, from her roofs when Verrio's colours fall,
And leave inanimate the naked wall,
Still in thy song should vanquish'd France appear,
And bleed for ever under Britain's spear.

Philips was the precursor of the eloquent school of descriptive poets who favoured blank verse, we must give Ambrose Philips the credit of having been the first poet of the eighteenth century who thought of using the uniformly correct couplet for depicting unusual aspects of nature with precise observation. He owes the distinction to his single piece in this vein, the description of a stretch of country in Denmark ice-bespangled by a sudden frost after rain, entitled *Epistle to the Earl of Dorset, Copenhagen, March 9, 1709*, from which we may quote the following lines:

> For every shrub, and every blade of grass,
> And every pointed thorn, seem'd wrought in glass;
> In pearls and rubies rich the hawthorns show,
> While through the ice the crimson berries glow.
> The thick-sprung reeds, which watery marshes yield,
> Seem'd polish'd lances in a hostile field.
> The stag, in limpid currents, with surprise,
> Sees crystal branches on his forehead rise:
> The spreading oak, the beech, and towering pine,
> Glaz'd over, in the freezing ether shine.
> The frighted birds the rattling branches shun,
> Which wave and glitter in the distant sun.
> When if a sudden gust of wind arise,
> The brittle forest into atoms flies,
> The crackling wood beneath the tempest bends,
> And in a spangled shower the prospect ends.

The freshness and originality of such a poem could not fail to win contemporary recognition, especially when the picture was conveyed in the form of a polite verse epistle; and Pope in one of his first letters commended it as 'a very lively piece of poetical painting,' while Steele in *The Tatler* proclaimed it to be 'as fine a piece as we ever had from any of the schools of the most learned painters; such images as these give us a new pleasure in our sight; and fix upon our minds traces of reflection which accompany us whenever the like objects occur.' The ability to write with eye on the object, which is manifest in these lines, justifies us in inquiring whether a similar sensitiveness to natural beauty may not be discerned in his *Pastorals*, where the language of artifice is of necessity employed.

Their appearance in Tonson's *Miscellany* of May 1709

together with the *Pastorals* of Pope invited some discrimination between the two, particularly as the style of Pope's
bucolics inclined to Virgilian elegance, while those of
Philips showed a leaning towards Spenserian rusticity.
During the spring of 1713, Tickell contributed a series of
papers to *The Guardian* in which, though no comparisons
were drawn, Philips's *Pastorals* were praised for their sup-
posedly rustic qualities and for their adoption of English
names, flowers, and proverbs in the place of classical ones,
while Pope—who, as we have seen, set himself to suggest
English landscapes without departing from neo-classical
convention—was somewhat pointedly ignored. If a less
touchy man than Pope might have taken offence at this,
no one but Pope could have retaliated in the manner he
devised for the purpose. Maintaining the style of airy
eulogy which had been employed in these essays, he anony-
mously contributed a final paper to the series, in which,
with the alleged purpose of justifying the foregoing neglect
of Pope's *Pastorals*, he mercilessly ridiculed Philips's
flutings by praising his worst passages, and by proclaiming
their superiority to his own finest lines. 'Mr. Pope,' he said,
'hath fallen into the same error with Virgil.' He extolled
Philips as 'the eldest born of Spenser, and our only true
Arcadian' on account of his 'beautiful rusticity,' and illustrated the latter with the couplet:

'O woeful day! O day of woe, quoth he,
And woeful I, who live the day to see!'

'That simplicity of diction,' he added, 'the melancholy
flowing of the numbers, the solemnity of the sound, and the
easy turn of the words, in this dirge (to make use of our
author's expression) are extremely elegant.' It is said that
when Steele received the paper, he failed to detect its irony,
and being unwilling that a fellow-contributor should suffer,
showed it to Pope, who, however, affected magnanimity and
urged him to publish it. On its appearance, Philips was so
enraged that he hung up a birch rod in Button's, and swore
that if Pope visited the club again, he would use it on his
person. The story, which has been related by almost every-
one who has written about Pope's early career, from Johnson's time to the present, gains additional point from the fact

that in his letter, referred to above, Pope bestowed high (though not unqualified) praise on Philips's *Pastorals*, and that in 1735 he considerably diminished this praise when preparing the letter for publication.

But allowing for the tortuous shifts of Pope's malevolence, and subtracting, as far as is possible, the element of personal rancour, we can still find sufficient traces of consistency between the letter and the paper, and enough just censure in the paper itself, to be able to infer what were Pope's genuine views on the quality of these poems. In the letter, he observed that the first pastoral was the best, and the second the worst; with regard to the fifth, which contains a skilful and elaborate description by 'Cuddy' of a musical contest between a swain and a nightingale, he remarked 'nothing can be objected but that [these lines] are too lofty for pastoral, especially being put into the mouth of a shepherd, as they are here; in the poet's own person they had been, I believe, more proper. These are more after Virgil's manner than that of Theocritus, whom yet in the character of pastoral he rather seems to imitate.'[1] In his *Guardian* essay he barely alludes to the first piece, but trounces the second on account of its sham simplicity and the banality of its proverbs (such as 'A stone rolling is ever bare of moss'), while he illustrates the element of incongruity, which he had noticed in the fifth, with additional examples drawn from the preceding pastorals. In both pieces of criticism the affectedly simple manner (a besetting weakness of Philips, which later earned him his nickname of 'namby-pamby'[2]) is condemned outright, while the more elevated, polished style is held to be out of place unless (as in Pope's own *Pastorals*) it is skilfully sustained throughout. If therefore we may interpret Pope's censure as being chiefly directed against the mixture of styles apparent in these poems, it cannot be doubted that the charge is a just one. For in a highly artificial form, such as the pastoral, a certain consistency of texture is necessary if the effect of idyllic fantasy is to be maintained. Philips's artistry is seen at its best in

[1] Letter to H. Cromwell, October 28, 1710. The *motif* of the shepherd-nightingale contest was probably derived either from a Latin poem by Strada, or from an English rendering (entitled *Music's Duel*) by Crashaw.

[2] It was probably bestowed on him by Swift, who parodied his verses on children, and who on political grounds resented his presence in Ireland.

detached passages; but as a whole his *Pastorals* lack imaginative coherence.

In quoting from the latter we will do well to choose such examples as show various ways of felicitously subordinating nature to the idiom of the neo-classic pastoral. First let us take a passage from the musical contest between the shepherd and the nightingale, referred to above. Here it will be seen that any actuality of underlying experience which may have prompted the strains is almost entirely subdued to the element of melodious virtuosity.

> He draws-in breath, his rising breath to fill:
> Throughout the wood his pipe is heard to shrill.
> From note to note, in haste, his fingers fly;
> Still more and more the numbers multiply:
> And now they trill, and now they fall and rise,
> And swift and slow they change with sweet surprise.
> Attentive she doth scarce the sounds retain;
> But to herself first cons the puzzling strain,
> And tracing, heedful, note by note repays
> The shepherd in his own harmonious lays,
> Through every changing cadence runs at length,
> And adds in sweetness what she wants in strength.

Though the lines do not of themselves suggest that Philips had listened to a nightingale or had done more than compare the modulations of poetic with those of actual music, yet it may be said that with the help of their agreeable pastoral setting they persuade the reader to think of the nightingale as a bird somewhat more than as, say, an oboe echoing the strains of a flute. They cannot however quite compare in either musical or suggestive qualities with a similar passage from Pope's *Winter* beginning:

> No more the birds shall imitate her lays.

This line, it is interesting to note, Pope changed in his manuscript to:

> No more the nightingales repeat her lays

but restored the original reading, after Philips's *Pastorals* had appeared, in order to avoid too close a resemblance.

If however we require evidence that Philips was capable of treating nature in a more objective manner, we could hardly choose a better example than is provided by the

opening and concluding lines of the sixth pastoral. The
latter is, in substance, a song-contest between two shepherds,
and contains verses of serene and tranquil beauty such as:

> Breathe soft, ye winds; ye waters, gently flow;
> Shield her, ye trees; ye flowers, around her grow:
> Ye swains, I beg you, pass in silence by;
> My love, in yonder vale, asleep does lie.

Here it can sooner be felt than demonstrated, that the poet
has drawn on memories of rural scenes enjoyed; and it
may be remarked that as if to atone for the generalized
character of such lyrical interchanges he frames them in
a somewhat distinctly visualized setting of sea-cliffs and
grazing herds.

> How still the sea behold! how calm the sky!
> And how, in sportive chase, the swallows fly!
> My goats, secure from harm, small tendance need,
> While high, on yonder hanging rock, they feed:
> And here below, the banky shore along,
> Your heifers graze.

The illusion of precise locality is increased by the depiction
of the same scene towards the close of day, when the singing-
bout is over:

> A mizzling mist descends
> Adown that steepy rock: and this way tends
> Yon distant rain. Shoreward the vessels strive;
> And, see, the boys their flocks to shelter drive.

These lines, we may note, show some resemblance to the
conclusion of Pope's *Winter*, where the 'unwholesome dews'
descend and the shade of the pines deepens. But the settings
of Pope's *Pastorals* are less direct, more diffused, and, as
has been shown in regard to the *Summer* especially, require a
rarer kind of artistry than that employed in the compara-
tively naturalistic example we have given from Philips.
It is true that in his Discourse on *Pastoral Poetry* Pope holds
that in each eclogue 'a designed scene or prospect is to be
presented to our view, which should likewise have its
variety.' He adds however that 'this variety is obtained in a
great degree by frequent comparisons, drawn from the most
agreeable objects of the country.' When Philips resorts to
the depiction of rural beauty by means of similes he is apt
to produce his happiest lines:

Soft falling as the still, refreshing dew,
To slake the drought, and herbage to renew:
Not half so sweet the midnight winds, which move
In drowsy murmurs o'er the waving grove,
Nor valley brook, that, hid by alders, speeds
O'er pebbles warbling, and through whispering reeds.

Observation is present in these comparisons, but it is unobtrusive, and the descriptive digression is attuned to the prevailing mood of the pastoral; conventional poetic terms are freely used, yet by a touch here and there, and the skilful interplay of vowel music, the lines acquire the kind of animation which diffuses its effect over the whole. It is when writing in this vein that Philips most nearly approaches the level of Pope's art-concealing art, and in doing so further exemplifies our contention that in poetry of the 'artificial' kind, an ability to depict objects with precision is a necessary condition of the power to generalize successfully.

CHAPTER VII

John Philips (1676–1708)

IN considering the work of any individual from among
the host of eighteenth-century imitators of Milton,
one may start with an almost insurmountable prejudice against the practice of pilfering the outward features
of the great style in the service of mere elegance. But in
order to mitigate this aversion, we should be prepared to
allow that Milton 'higher sang, but gave them breath.'
Milton's language, as was first shown by Philips, could
without debasement be applied to the treatment of a whole
range of homely or familiar subjects such as agriculture,
hunting, or the rules of health, provided there was frequently
present a sense of half-humorous relish in the process of
applying a highly-wrought classical style to the depiction of
everyday objects, and provided some small but unmistakable
poetic gain accrued as the result of so large a borrowing.
It is the task of criticism to separate the profitable from
the insolvent, to give their due to those poets who show some
liveliness of fancy in adapting the Miltonic language to
novel or not normally 'poetic' subjects, and to those in
whom (unsubdued to the 'disgusting solemnity of manner'
which Goldsmith aptly deprecated in the later and more
lifeless imitators) the Miltonic vein releases an original
poetic faculty of description or reflection, which might
otherwise have remained inarticulate. It should be borne in
mind also, that the majority of the eighteenth-century
writers of blank verse had no wish to stray outside the 'walled
garden' of Augustanism; they set before themselves the
classical ideals of propriety, order, and balance, and we must
estimate them by what they set out to do, rather than stress
how near they sometimes approached, how often fell short
of other ideals of poetic achievement. To them, Milton's
blank verse and elaborate language presented a new and
untried medium for 'classical' self-expression; it was accordingly taken up and practised with eagerness, and a blank
verse school of poets grew up, not so much in opposition

to, as opposed by, the Pope school of regular coupletry.[1]

The most influential of the Miltonic pioneers was John Philips, in whose verse it is interesting to observe the transition from parody to complete imitation of Milton, surely one of the most fruitful ways in which a close discipleship may be developed. At first, he is fascinated by the capacity of the Miltonic style to dignify and transfigure whatever subjects it is confronted with (compare, in Milton himself, 'Tame villatic fowl,' 'no fear lest dinner cool' and the like), no less than by its triumphant management of poetic Latin constructions and classical allusions. The 'sensuous' element in Milton's verse was no doubt enhanced, for Philips, by the hair-combing, which we are told accompanied his readings of the poet, while he was at school. The author of the article on Philips in the *Biographia Britannica* states that he seldom joined in play with the boys, but :

> generally retired then to his chamber, where he procured a person to attend to him, and comb his hair, of which he had a very handsome flow. In this very singular recreation he felt an exquisite delight. . . . It was in these intervals chiefly that he read Milton; however, this was not before he was well acquainted with both Virgil and Homer, and the frequent imitations he found of these authors in *Paradise Lost*, falling in exactly with his own turn, hence he conceived an ardent passion for the English poet.

We may infer from this also that the classic poets held so high a place in his esteem, that he valued Milton chiefly for his ability to recapture their peculiar excellences of expression in his own verse. There is no reason to suppose that he did not subscribe to the current belief that 'To copy nature is to copy them,' and the manner of copying them (the ancients) being more convincingly displayed in Milton's poetry than that of Dryden or Pope, he forthwith set about the gratifying task of imitating Milton. The outcome of his apprenticeship is the engaging tour-de-force *The Splendid Shilling* (1701). A good parody, it is generally admitted, should show as much appreciation of the niceties as of the humorous potentialities of an author's style, and in *The Splendid Shilling* the two are adroitly combined. The

---

[1]Cf. Pope's Postscript to his translation of the *Odyssey*, and Johnson's views on blank verse in his *Life of Thomson* and elsewhere.

following extract displays something better than high-spirited exaggeration, there is an understanding of the fact that Milton's involved parentheses and prolonged similes are extended to a point determined not by the range of his erudition but by the demands of a complex and undulating rhythm. The collocation of proper names in the last line, where the special spelling enhances the musical effect, provides a redoubtable close to the period. The poet's occupation in his penurious condition is to:

> . . . doze at home
> In garret vile, and with a warming puff
> Regale chill'd Fingers; or from Tube as black
> As Winter-Chimney, or well-polish'd jet,
> Exhale *Mundungus*, ill-perfuming Scent;
> Not blacker Tube, nor of a shorter Size
> Smoaks *Cambro-Britain* (vers'd in Pedigree,
> Sprung from *Cadwalader* and *Arthur*, Kings
> Full famous in Romantic tale) when he
> O'er many a craggy Hill, and barren Cliff,
> Upon a Cargo of fam'd *Cestrian* Cheese,
> High over-shadowing rides, with a design
> To vend his Wares, or at th' *Arvonian* Mart,
> Or *Maridunum*, or the ancient Town
> Eclip'd *Brechinia*, or where *Vaga's* Stream
> Encircles Ariconium, fruitful Soil,
> Whence flow Nectareous Wines, that well may vye
> With *Massic*, *Setin*, or renown'd *Falern*.

The poem *Cyder* (1708) has an undeniable importance in literary history as the most considerable of the early imitations of Milton, as the first British *Georgic*,[1] and as the precursor of a long line of didactic or commercial epics. This historical value (which is all that Philips is commonly allowed) should not be overlooked even when we are attempting to estimate the absolute merits of the poem, since the gift of invention, if sufficiently pronounced (and Philips had a genius for adaptation that was almost equivalent to pure invention) shows a certain keenness of imagination, which can seldom be quite obscured by indifferent execution. The extravagant praises which were showered on Philips by poets of the first half of the eighteenth

[1] For reminiscences of the *Georgics*, cf. *Cyder* I, 741 sq. with *Georgics* II, 490 sq., and *Cyder* I, 321–5 with *Georgics* III, 375–84.

century, the translations of *Cyder* that were made, even the hostility of such writers as Gay[1] and Samuel Wesley, all show a widespread recognition that the author had opened up a new field for poetic craftsmanship. Nor, we may surmise, would he have acquired this notoriety if he had not in the eyes of his compeers excelled, at least intermittently, in actual performance.

It was surely a stroke of insight to perceive that the province of Augustan poetry could, with notable classical precedent, be extended beyond the walled garden to include the orchard. It showed further discernment to realize that, as the wielder of 'the stateliest measure ever moulded by the lips of man' had used that instrument to elevate a rural theme,[2] so the style of the great English bard, who was steeped in the poetry of the classics, could, if managed with subtlety and tact, be used for a similar purpose without offence. At all events the tributes to the fructifying idea are eloquent—if sometimes too much so—they consist of the long succession of discursive blank verse pieces of a didactic tendency, stretching from Thomson to Crabbe and Cowper and beyond. But for *Cyder* there might have been no *Seasons*, and without it even the 'divine chit-chat' of Cowper might not have come into being. The popularity and superior

---

[1]Gay did not consider the theme of *Cyder* elevated enough for a Georgic. He thought Ambrose Philips's Eclogues too artificial and John Philips's Georgics too tame.

[2]It is interesting to compare two opinions not unfairly representative of their respective centuries, concerning the nature of the diction employed by Virgil in the *Georgics*. W. Y. Sellar (*Virgil*, 1897) holds that 'Nothing shows the perfect sanity of Virgil's genius more clearly than his entire exemption from the besetting sin of the eighteenth century, that of calling common things by pompous names, and of dignifying trifles by applying heroic phrases to them.' Addison, on the other hand (*Essay on Virgil's Georgics*) in discussing 'the style proper to a Georgic' considered that the poet 'ought in particular to be careful of not letting his subject debase his style, and betray him into a meanness of expression, but everywhere to keep up his verse in all the pomp of numbers, and dignity of words,' and praised Virgil for adorning his expression 'with metaphors, Grecisms, and circumlocutions, to give his verse the greater pomp, and preserve it from sinking into a plebeian style. . . . He [Virgil] delivers the meanest of his precepts with a kind of grandeur, he breaks the clods and tosses the dung about with an air of gracefulness.'

A work that is capable of being admired, at different periods, for contradictory reasons, has a fair expectation of permanence. Philips, we may surmise, would have subscribed to Addison's view of the matter. A great deal depends, however (as it has been our purpose to show) on the way in which the pomp and periphrases are applied. Addison perceived that 'we receive more strong and lively ideas of things from his words, than we could have done from the objects themselves,' yet he does not succeed in reproducing this quality in his translation (of the fourth *Georgic*) to anything like the extent that Dryden does in his version; and the reason is partly because of Dryden's more discerning manipulation of the stock phraseology.

poetic merit of *The Seasons* largely eclipsed the fame of the earlier poem, but Thomson acknowledged his debt in *Autumn*, where the description of the mellow profusion of ripe fruits brings to his mind:

> Thy native theme, and boon inspirer too,
> Philips, Pomona's bard, the second thou
> Who nobly durst, in rhyme-unfettered verse,
> With British freedom sing the British song:

For the most part such general resemblances as exist between the two poems are those which they have in common with the *Georgics*, yet Thomson may have caught something of Philips's manner of veering off into seemingly random digressions, something of his style of arbitrarily introducing complimentary verses to his friends and patrons, and, of more account, some of his talent for attractively describing his works and days in accurate detail without lapsing into mere naturalism. A few of Thomson's outstanding passages, too, may be traced to their probable source in Philips; thus the expenditure of sympathy on the birds slaughtered by the sportsmen in *Autumn* (360–400) appears to have been suggested by the lines on the Fowler in *Cyder* II (173–6):

> Offensive to the Birds, sulphureous Death
> Checques their mid Flight, and heedless while they strain
> Their tuneful throats, the towring heavy lead
> O'er-takes their speed; they leave their little Lives
> Above the Clouds, praecipitant to Earth.

while the description of the drinking-bout in *Cyder* (II, 433 ff.) may well have provided Thomson with the hint for his unforgettable scene of conviviality after the hunt (*Autumn*, 502 ff.)—one of his rare interior *genre*-pictures.

When *The Seasons* was published, the influence of *Cyder* on it was at once recognized.

> Read Philips, much, consider Milton more;
> But from their dross extract the purer ore;

was the advice of Somerville, in his *Poetical Epistle upon the first edition of The Seasons*. So far as it is possible to compare the two poems, it may be said that *The Seasons* has the advantage over *Cyder* in not following Milton too closely; for however much Thomson may have emulated the grand style, his first concern was with the truthful reproduction of what he had seen and heard and felt, and he has the faculty of grafting his own expressions on to the formal poetic dialect, whenever the occasion serves. With Philips on the other hand there is little of this spontaneity, and we seldom lose the impression of a translation, of the task involved in dealing with unusually intractable material in an unsparingly elevated manner. The profusion of italicized proper names with which Philips considers it fitting to adorn his page (e.g., I, 580–95) in itself distinguishes him from Thomson, and brings to mind his own description of his manner of composition:

> . . . I all the live-long Day
> Consume in Meditation deep, recluse
> From human Converse, nor, at shut of Eve,
> Enjoy Repose; but oft at Midnight lamp
> Ply my brain-racking studies, if by chance
> Thee I may counsel right; and oft this Care
> Disturbs me slumbring.

It is perhaps as a result of his preoccupation with a learned style that his technical precepts concerning the cultivation of orchards and the preparation of the liquor rarely convey either the glamour which Virgil by almost imperceptible touches was able to infuse into an equally detailed treatment of farm life, or the sense of open-air participation in rural activities which Thomson with his more expansive manner was able to impart to his descriptions of sheep-shearing and trout-fishing. Though the subject-matter of *Cyder* is far more condensed than that of Thomson's poem, there is a certain verbosity about Philips's expression, an individual defect beyond the adopted mannerisms of style, which prevents him attaining Thomson's frequently sustained precision of effect.

This is not to deny, however, that Philips has many touches of original perception and felicitous expressions of natural beauty. He has an eye for landscape and, though far inferior to Thomson in this respect, some faculty for composing the objects of his vision into a harmonious whole. A good example is provided by the following lines, whose artistic integrity is indisputable:

Here to the Sight,
Apples of Price, and plenteous Sheaves of Corn,
Oft interlac'd occurr, and both imbibe
Fitting congenial Juice; so rich the Soil,
So much does fructuous Moisture o'er-abound!
Nor are the Hills unaimiable, whose Tops
To Heav'n aspire, affording Prospect sweet
To Human Ken; nor at their Feet the Vales
Descending gently, where the lowing Herd
Chews Verd'rous Pasture: nor the yellow Fields
Gaily enterchang'd, with rich Variety
Pleasing, as when an *Emerald* green, enchas'd
In flamy gold, from the bright Mass acquires
A nobler Hue, more delicate to Sight.

As we should expect to find, in any extract of moderate
length from Philips, there are patches here of both Miltonic
Latinism and Popian stock diction. Yet on regarding them
closely they will be found to enhance rather than blur the
total effect. The word 'fructuous' suggests a relish in the
cause of the rich and smiling fertility that gladdens the eye;
the function of the Latin double negative in 'Nor are the
Hills unaimiable' is not one of mere elegance, for the
contrived understatement suggests some of the unpreten-
tious charm of the landscape; the conventional phrase 'lowing
Herd,' placed where it is, besides completing the verbal
melody of the line, adds a touch of variety to the picture at
the right point and contributes to the depiction of the typical
configurations of a Herefordshire valley; while the jewelry
simile at the end of the passage, conventionally exception-
able on the grounds that Augustan diction, by reason of its
town origin, draws too much from objects of dress or ornament, yet serves its purpose in sharpening the recollection
of the dazzling contrasts of colour that are produced by
bright sunshine on fields in bloom.

Less directly pictorial, but, like Thomson's subdued
effects, suggestive in their undertones of mingled scents
and sounds, the following lines convey something of the
cool serenity of an early morning in autumn:

Autumn paints
Ausonian Hills with Grapes, whilst English Plains
Blush with pomaceous Harvests, breathing Sweets.
O let me now, when the kind early Dew

Unlocks th' embosom'd Odours, walk among
The well rang'd Files of Trees, whose full-ag'd Store
Diffuse *Ambrosial* Steams, than *Myrrh,* or *Nard*
More grateful, or perfuming flow'ry Beane!
Soft whisp'ring Airs, and the larks mattin Song
Then woo to musing, and becalm the Mind
Perplex'd with irksome thoughts.

Here, on a rigorous analysis the phrases 'Blush with pomaceous Harvests' and 'Diffuse Ambrosial Steams' would be pointed to as instances of unnecessary rotundity; but they are, after all, only mild examples of the prevailing idiom, and since they contribute musically to the rest of the passage, they pass unchallenged in the reading.

Before taking leave of Philips there is another aspect of his art that deserves recognition, both on its own merits and on account of its considerable influence on succeeding writers of blank verse poems. Philips begun his poetic career, as has been seen, with broad parody; he ended it with studiously-contrived imitation. There is, it is true, a passage in *Cyder*, describing the unpleasant shock of eating a grub-infested apple, where the poet without the slightest compunction relapses into pure burlesque and emphasizes the effect by a 'ludicrous' simile. Usually, however, he does not depend on extravagances of this sort when he wishes to lighten his verse; instead, he resorts to a slight playfulness of manner in which, while the object or situation is described without distortion, the whimsical effects of the conjunction of the dignified style and the homely theme are subtly brought out. Passages of this kind are seen most advantageously in their own context, since they depend for the element of surprise on their contrast with the surrounding style. Philips has a number of these describing the various pests to which the orchards are subject—birds, snails, wasps, pigs;—the injunctions concerning how to deal with the latter may be quoted:

> Besides, the filthy Swine will oft invade
> Thy firm Inclosure, and with delving Snout
> The rooted Forest undermine: forthwith
> Alloo thy furious Mastiff, bid him vex
> The noxious Herd, and print upon their Ears
> A sad Memorial of their past Offence.

We may trace this vivid yet elevated manner of writing from Philips, through Thomson, and up to Cowper; without it English blank verse would have been the poorer.

WILLIAM SHENSTONE

To those who are inclined to look with more condescension than sympathy on the productions of eighteenth-century minor poets, Shenstone presents an easy opportunity for semi-humorous belittlement. Though corpulent in form, he posed in his songs and ballads as a sprightly 'Damon of the plain;' though content to be regarded as a herald of Little Romanticism, he was lymphatic and unadventurous in disposition—his most marked departure from convention being the wearing of 'his own hair' instead of a wig[1]—his literary interests were petty and restricted, he was unsuccessful in love, and through indolence and neglect ran himself into debt. Moreover a lifetime spent in pottering about his estate and adorning it with inscribed urns and obelisks, waterfalls and 'vistos,' did not stave off his own ennui or fail to provide occasion for the contemptuous comments of fellow-dilettantes and more weighty persons alike. Thus Gray, in a letter, remarked 'Poor Shenstone, why does he not do better? He hops round his walks and is afraid to venture beyond his line . . . His whole philosophy consisted in living, against his will, in a retirement which his taste had adorned; but which he only enjoyed when people of note came to see and commend it.' Horace Walpole, seemingly unaware that similar taunts might be aimed at himself and strike nearer the mark, exclaimed 'Poor man! He wanted to have all the world talk of him for the pretty place he had made, and which he seems to have made only that it might be talked of.' And Dr. Johnson, who was inveterately hostile to cultured *fainéants*, fabricated a story of how parties of visitors to the Leasowes were perversely conducted by amateur guides to 'inconvenient points of

[1]'. . . However a peruke may tend to soften the human features it can very seldom make amends for the mixture of artifice which it discovers.'—*Essay on Dress.*

view' and the wrong ends of walks; and observed drily of the mildly fastidious owner that 'his life was unstained by any crime.'

Though in some respects these reflections present a fairly true image of the man, they do not detract from the fact that he introduced into nature-poetry a vein of sentiment peculiarly his own, and that he skilfully employed the resources of artificial imagery and metrical variety in order to give it a persuasive and graceful form of expression. He observed in Spenser 'a peculiar tenderness of sentiment remarkable throughout his works,' and his readiness of fancy, together with his feeling for nuances of rhythm, enabled him to produce, in *The Schoolmistress*, one of the most successful Spenserian imitations of the age. In Spenser the visionary adventures of the days of chivalry took on at times the kind of mild and sunny glamour which Shenstone attributed, in retrospect, to the archaic and self-contained world of the Halesowen dame-school. It was through this correspondence of mood that he was able to reproduce so well the 'beautiful redundance' of Spenser's terminal alexandrine; as for example in his reminiscence of the cottage-garden on Sunday evenings:

> Sweet melody! to hear her then repeat
> How Israel's sons, beneath a foreign king,
> While taunting foemen did a song entreat,
> All for the nonce untuning every string,
> Uphung their useless lyres—small heart had they to sing.

He had also a 'winter-mood,' when his livelier poetic impulse gave place to a moral and reflective strain; but his meditations in this key are seen to better advantage in his disconnected observations (in prose) *On Men and Manners* than in his versified *Moral Pieces* and Elegies where, except for a few well-turned stanzas, such as:

> Vain now are books, the sage's widom vain!
> What has the world to bribe our steps astray?
> Ere Reason learns by studied laws to reign,
> The weaken'd passions, self-subdued, obey.

his talent for succinctness of phrase deserts him.

His nature-poetry of unquestionable merit is to be found (amongst several pieces that hardly rise above mediocrity) in the ode *Rural Elegance*, in a handful of inscriptions, and in a few pastoral songs and ballads. The latter, in particular, have not lacked admirers; Mr. I. A. Williams, who has written on Shenstone with knowledge and discernment, holds them to be 'the best things of their kind in the English language, which is not very rich in that sort of poetry,' while Charles Lamb declared 'the true rustic style, the Arcadian English, I think, is to be found in Shenstone.' His lyrical lightness and grace comes most refreshingly after one has become accustomed to the more measured and deliberate strains of *The Seasons*, just as The Leasowes is best appreciated after a visit to the more ample parklands of Hagley. As he observed in his *Essay on Elegy*; 'Wealth and splendour will never want their proper weight: the danger is lest they should too much preponderate. A kind of poetry, therefore, which throws its chief influence into the other scale . . . may chance to please.'

It may almost be said that for full appreciation his lyrical poems require to be visualized in their local landscape setting. This for two reasons; in the first place his fancy was quickened by 'the habitual scene of hill and dale' and his interests were bounded by his *ferme ornée*—as can be seen from his proclivity for drawing comparisons from gardening in his essays, e.g.:

> A large retinue upon a small income, like a large cascade upon a small stream, tends to discover its tenuity.

and:

> I hate a style, as I do a garden, that is wholly flat and regular; that slides along like an eel, and never rises to what one can call an inequality.

Secondly, his extraordinary capacity for visual composition was so fully absorbed by his landscape-gardening that he refrained, wisely, from attempting to depict in words what had already been perfectly achieved by the planting of trees, the planning of walks and the winding of waters. His poems exhibit a succession of rural images that are addressed to the ear rather than the eye, but there is no doubting the closeness of their association, in sentiment, with the surroundings amongst which they were composed. As he points out in the *Essay on Elegy*:

If he describes a rural landskip, or unfolds the train of sentiments it inspired,[1] he fairly drew his picture from the spot; and
felt very sensibly the affection he communicates. If he speaks of
his humble shed, his flocks and his fleeces, he does not counterfeit
the scene . . . The flocks, the meadows and the grottoes are
his own, and the embellishment of his farm his sole amusement.
As the sentiments, therefore, were inspired by Nature, and that
in the earlier part of his life, he hopes they will retain a natural
appearance.

For detailed descriptions of The Leasowes, the reader must
be referred to R. Dodsley's beguiling guide to the estate
(included, with a folding map, in the second volume of his
edition of Shenstone's collected works, 1764) and to the
more modern accounts of Hugh Miller and E. M. Purkis.
We may observe here, however, that Shenstone so successfully applied William Kent's guiding principle—'Nature
abhors a straight line'—to the concurring contours of his
estate that one of his eulogists was moved to exclaim:

> Yon stream that wanders down the dale,
> The spiral wood, the winding vale,
> The path which, wrought with hidden skill,
> Slow twining scales yon distant hill
> With fir invested—all combine
> To recommend the WAVING LINE.

If he did not entirely refrain from what Thomas Warton
called 'the pedantry of vegetation,' he avoided the more
freakish accessories of landscape ornament which were often
to be met with in the latter part of the century. The 'ruinated
priory' which he built near his lake (still standing but now
decidedly over-ruinated) was at least untenanted by an
artificial hermit.[2] In the *Unconnected Thoughts on Gardening*
his various schemes for landscape grouping are qualified by
frequent assertions as to the importance of preventing
natural beauty from being spoilt by artifice:

> The eye requires a sort of balance here; but not so as to en-
> croach upon probable nature. A wood, or hill, may balance a
> house or obelisk; for exactness would be displeasing.

[1] The first of these activities (in the usual sense) he never practises; the second he
employs constantly.
[2] This individual was pleasantly ridiculed in *Columella* by Shenstone's lifelong
friend, Richard Graves, who might be called the Peacock of Little Romanticism.
Cf. his account of the secret overturning of Shenstone's garden statuary by Mr.
Geoffry Wildgoose (with an illustration of the scene) in his novel *The Spiritual
Quixote.*

He carried out, in fact, Pope's sovereign principle of taste—
'Consult the genius of the place in all'—and it is for this reason
that his glades and dingles even today, when they retain
hardly a trace of his embellishments, readily encourage the
visitor to recapture the spirit in which his nature-lyrics
were written. 'Virgil's grove' no longer boasts its inscribed
obelisk, Thomson's seat, high waterfall and bathing Venus,
yet the stream still darts and glides beneath a canopy of
shade, through mossy banks sprinkled with wild flowers,
spreading into small sheets which catch the sunbeams and
sparkle to the eye.

Perhaps, then, it is not wholly fanciful to associate the
anapaestic rhythm of Shenstone's 'diploma-piece,' the
Pastoral Ballad, with the joyous tumbling and rippling of
his shyly sequestered brooks:

> I seldom have met with a loss,
> Such health do my fountains bestow;
> My fountains all border'd with moss,
> Where the harebells and violets grow.
>
> .   .   .   .   .
>
> Not a brook that is limpid and clear
> But it glitters with fishes of gold.

The metre was not new to eighteenth-century verse, for the
prototype of this ballad may be seen in Rowe's *Colin's
Complaint*, but it was owing to Shenstone that the pastoral
love-lyric in continuous anapaests became a popular form of
verse. In the hands of his imitators the themes are often
trivial and the lilt is apt to become monotonous, but Shenstone's piece is kept clear of these defects through the
sincerity of the underlying feeling. There is no doubting
the personal note in the following stanza, yet the poignancy
of the experience is successfully transmuted to favour and
prettiness:

> Alas! from the day that we met,
> What hope of an end to my woes?
> When I cannot endure to forget
> The glance that undid my repose.
> Yet time may diminish the pain:
> The flower, and the shrub, and the tree,
> Which I rear'd for her pleasure in vain,
> In time may have comfort for me.

Similarly the glimpses of nature disclosed in the ballad do not provide a mere decorative background; instead, the emotion is expressed through the picture given, as for instance in the joyfully expectant strains of *Hope* (the second division of the poem):

> Not a pine in the grove is there seen,
> But with tendrils of woodbine is bound;
> Not a beech's more beautiful green
> But a sweetbriar entwines it around:
>
> .   .   .   .   .
>
> O how sudden the jessamine strove
> With the lilac to render it gay!
> Already it calls for my love
> To prune the wild branches away.

That Shenstone had something of the field-naturalist's faculty of observation can be gathered from occasional touches such as the following, from *A Pastoral Ode*:

> Grieved him to lurk the lakes beside,
> Where coots in rushy dingles hide,
>   And moorcocks shun the day;
> While caitiff bitterns, undismay'd,
> Remark the swain's familiar shade,
>   And scorn to quit their prey.

His special and characteristic talent, however, lay in culling Arcadian suggestions from rural sights and sounds, and in making them contribute to the spell of his pastoral fantasies. The ultimate aim of his landscape-gardening, as he expressed it in *Rural Elegance*:

> To catch soft hints from Nature's tongue,
> And bid Arcadia bloom around.

was not, after all, so far removed from that of his poetry. We see the two activities happily combined in some of his inscriptions on seats and urns, notably in that beginning:

> Here, in cool grot and mossy cell,
> We rural fays and fairies dwell;

—lines which are well suited to the spirit of the place (a miniature gorge with a playfully-eddying stream, just below Virgil's grove).

The ode *Rural Elegance*, referred to above, may be

regarded as Shenstone's versified *apologia*[1]. It is persuasively, if somewhat diffusely written, and contains (among other vignettes of comparable merit) a passage in which the delight afforded by scenes of summer ripeness and profusion is effectively communicated. He demands of the husbandmen:

> But though the various harvest gild your plains,
> Does the mere landscape feast your eye?
> Or the warm hope of distant gains
> Far other cause of glee supply?
> Is not the red-streak's future juice
> The source of your delight profound,
> Where Ariconium pours her gems profuse,
> Purpling a whole horizon round?

In this we may notice, as characteristic of Shenstone's aptitude for *nuances* of expression, how the understatement in 'Far other cause of glee supply' enhances the note of tranquil and meditative delight, and how the lingering movement of the last line suggests a fondly evoked recollection of far-stretching expanses of foliage and colour.

In encouraging Cunningham to write in the pastoral vein, Shenstone seems to have passed on some of his special talent to the younger poet, who shows an almost equal grace and dexterity in handling the anapaestic lyric and in combining, to mutual advantage, stock phrases with original imagery. Cunningham's descriptive verse, however, exhibits an interesting contrast to Shenstone's in that the latter secures his effects mainly by means of musical suggestion, while the former has a keen eye for both outline and *chiaroscuro*. That he uses this gift discriminatingly, and in the service of a poetical rather than a pictorial impression, may be seen in the piece called *A Landscape*. His artistry is equally apparent in his best poem, *Day*, where a number of small pictures, each complete in itself, such as:

> From the low-roof'd cottage ridge,
> See the chatt'ring Swallow spring;

[1] The defence of his dilettantism is seen to best advantage in the following lines:—
> And sure there seem, of human kind,
>   Some born to shun the solemn strife;
> Some for amusive tasks design'd,
>   To soothe the certain ills of life;
> Grace its lone vales with many a budding rose,
> New founts of bliss disclose,
> Call forth refreshing shades, and decorate repose.

> Darting through the one-arch'd bridge,
> Quick she dips her dappled wing.

are presented in temporal rather than spatial succession. The poem with its three divisions, Morning, Noon, and Evening, has an almost Blake-like simplicity and freshness, and it owes its distinctive quality largely to the readiness with which these sharply-defined, yet swift and lyrical delineations compose into a final unity of impression. In spite of differences of technique, Shenstone and Cunningham are associated through similarity of mood and poetic impulse. Both had a capacity for deriving a keen and uncloying pleasure from small and secluded pastoral scenes, and both communicate their pleasure in verse which has lightness and simplicity without being insipid. The sensibility required for this kind of attainment is one which betokens a full realization of Shenstone's precept:

> Shepherd, wouldst thou here obtain
> Pleasure unalloy'd with pain?
> Joy that suits the rural sphere?
> Gentle shepherd, lend an ear.
> Learn to relish calm delight.

To-day, the miniature Arcadias which gladdened these eighteenth-century poets are apt to fall a prey to urban developments, and The Leasowes in particular is threatened by the encroachments of the Black Country in a way that makes one recall—with more regret than moral approval—the intrusion of Sir Industry into the pleasant embowering retreats of the Castle of Indolence.

CONCLUSION

The four poets treated above may appear to have been somewhat arbitrarily chosen, and it is true that their selection has been partly governed by personal preference. But they have been included also because they are generally undervalued as nature-poets, and because their work shows in individual ways the characteristics—visual composition and the creative use of conventional phraseology—whose importance we had previously urged by means of theoretical discussion and incidental illustration. If by suggesting a more sympathetic manner of approach to eighteenth-century descriptive poetry (whether of the eclogue or georgic type) we have encouraged further exploration of the kind, our purpose may be held to have succeeded. One or two poets may perhaps be mentioned whose work, neglected except by a few, deserves to be better known and liked. The 'bard of the Fleece,' for example; whose *Grongar Hill* has diverted admiration from his chief poem. The latter, no doubt, like many poems of the kind, is of unequal merit and excessive length. Yet in its own day it received the discerning praise of Akenside and Scott of Amwell, while Wordsworth, who had a more catholic taste than some of the neo-Romantic critics, paid a warm tribute to its 'living landscape fair and bright.' Dyer takes an equal pride in the rich fleeces of English sheep and the beauty of their pastures:

> The food of wool
> Is grass or herbage soft, that ever blooms
> In temperate air, in the delicious downs
> Of Albion, on the banks of all her streams.

Parnell, one of the early Augustan nature-poets, whose descriptive powers Johnson recalled when viewing the scenery of North Wales, has also his special claims to wider recognition. A zealous admirer of Pope's *Windsor Forest* and of Milton's early poems, his borrowings from these sources do not diminish his originality, as may be seen notably in his *Health, an Eclogue*. The *Night Piece on Death*, with its lake-side scene, shows his talent for visual composition, while in his moral *conte*, *The Hermit*, particular effects are often secured through generalized language, as in the couplet:

> There by the moon through ranks of trees they pass,
> Whose verdure crown'd their sloping sides of grass

—where the plurals with their full umbrageous whisper help to bring a landscape before the inward eye. Nor should Crowe be forgotten, whose *Lewesdon Hill*—a topographical poem of singular charm and fidelity to local appearances— was praised by both Wordsworth and Coleridge. James

Hurdis's *Village Curate* and *Favourite Village* sufficiently reward the reader who is not deterred by the worthy parson's over-zealous attempts to moralize in the manner of Cowper; as may be seen from the following example of his capacity for observant roving:

> I love to meet
> A sudden turn like this, which stops me short,
> Extravagantly devious, and invites
> Or up the hill or down; then winds again,
> By reeling drunkard trod, and sudden ends
> In a green swarded wain-way, not unlike
> Cathedral aisle completely roof'd with boughs,
> Which stretching up-hill through the gloomy wood
> Displays at either end a giant door
> Wide open'd.

Thomas Gisborne's *Walks in a Forest* (1794) also deserves to recover some of its lost popularity. Like Hurdis the author was a devoted admirer of Cowper, but his more massive style and his fondness for shifting atmospheric effects show that he took Thomson as his chief guide. Bowles, the last of the hill-poets, and the sonneteer who emulated Thomas Warton and inspired the youthful Coleridge, is usually allowed a place in the history of pre-romanticism on account of his endeavour 'to harmonize the moods of nature with those of the mind,' but he is to be valued also for his purely descriptive talent.

With these poets, Popian or Miltonic diction may occasionally result in empty elegance or grandiosity, but it is more often a means to the securing of skilful generalization of the pastoral type or the effective marshalling of visual detail. There was a wealth of good nature-poetry in the eighteenth century, and we are apt to find the rural spirit animating not only 'descriptive' verse but also the poetical treatises on hop-gardens, the rules of health, the chase and kindred subjects, whose semi-technical character too often keeps readers away. In appreciating the poetry of the period, we should try to recover, at least in part, the standpoint of the discerning contemporary reader. The qualities which were then perceived almost instinctively, now need to be pointed out, defined, and seen against their special background of convention. This kind of exposition we have attempted to provide, and it is hoped that in doing so we have helped to prepare the way for a higher general estimate of eighteenth-century nature-poetry than has prevailed hitherto.